LONDON TRAVEL GUIDE

The opportunity to explore the iconic landmarks of London.

PAUL A. MILLER

Copyright © 2024 by Paul A. Miller

All rights reserved. No part of this publication may be reproduced, distributed, or transmitted in any form or by any means, including photocopying, recording, or other electronic or mechanical methods, without the prior written permission of the publisher, except in the case of brief quotations embodied in critical reviews and certain other noncommercial uses permitted by copyright law.

Table of Contents

Introduction	**5**
Welcome to London	13
Why Visit London?	20
How to Use This Guide	25
Chapter 1:. Planning Your Trip	**32**
Best Time to Visit	39
Budgeting Your Trip	44
Travel Insurance	50
Essential Travel Apps	55
Chapter 2 Gettingto London	**62**
Entry Requirements	68
Chapter 3:Getting Around	**75**
Public Transport	82
London Underground (Tube)	90
Buses	96
Trams	102
River Services	107
Taxis and Ride-Sharing	113
Cycling	119
Walking Tours	124
Accessibility Tips	129
Chapter 4: Where to Stay	**137**
Neighbourhoods and Districts	143
Central London	149
West End	154
South Bank	160

East London	165
North London	170
West London	176
Types of Accommodation	182
Chapter 5:Top Attractions	**189**
The Tower of London	195
Buckingham Palace	196
Westminster Abbey	198
Houses of Parliament and Big Ben	199
Museums and Galleries	200
The British Museum	201
National Gallery	203
Tate Modern	204
Natural History Museum	205
Parks and Gardens	206
Hyde Park	213
Kew Gardens	214
Regent's Park	217
Hampstead Heath	218
Modern Attractions	219
The Shard	224
London Eye	225
Millennium Bridge	226
The O2	227
Chapter 6:Culture and Entertainment	**228**
Theatres and Performances	234
West End Shows	239
Shakespeare's Globe	241
Music and Concerts	244

Art and Exhibitions	251
Major Art Galleries	255
Street Art Tours	261
Festivals and Events	264
Christmas Markets	267
Chapter 7: Food and Drink	**270**
Traditional British Cuisine	273
International Flavors	276
Food Markets	280
Chapter:8 Shopping	**288**
Famous Shopping Streets	291
Chapter 9: Day Trips from London	**299**
Windsor	303
Oxford	304
Cambridge	305
Bath	306
Stonehenge	307
Brighton	308
Chapter 10: Practical Information	**309**
Chapter 11:Useful Phrases	**314**
British Slang and Idioms	318
Chapter 12:. Maps and Guides	**322**
City Map	325

Introduction

In the quiet town of Pinegrove, where life moved at a gentle pace, there lived a young woman named Emma. Emma was an avid reader, often found lost in the pages of books that transported her to distant lands and eras. Her favorite place in the world was the tiny bookshop on Elm Street, run by the kind and eccentric Mr. Whitaker. The shop, filled with the scent of aged paper and leather, was a sanctuary for Emma.

One rainy afternoon, seeking refuge from the drizzling rain, Emma stepped into the bookshop. As she browsed the shelves, a particular book caught her eye. Its cover was a deep, rich blue with intricate gold lettering that read, "The Enchanted Traveler: A Guide to London." Intrigued, she pulled the book from the shelf and dusted off its cover. The pages felt strangely warm under her fingertips.

Mr. Whitaker appeared from behind a stack of books, his eyes twinkling. "Ah, you've found a special one," he said. "That book has a bit of magic in it. They say it can take you places."

Emma smiled, thinking it was just another of Mr. Whitaker's whimsical stories. Nonetheless, she purchased the book and hurried home, eager to explore its contents. She settled into her favourite reading chair by the window, the rain tapping gently against the glass, and opened the book.

The first page was an illustration of London, with its iconic landmarks beautifully sketched. As she turned to the next page, she felt a strange sensation, like a gentle pull. The room around her began to blur and spin, and before she could react, everything went dark.

When Emma opened her eyes, she was no longer in her cozy reading nook. She was standing in the middle of Trafalgar Square, surrounded by the hustle and bustle of London. The sounds of the city, the chirping of birds, and the chatter of people filled her ears. She looked down and saw she was wearing a classic 19th-century dress, complete with a bonnet and gloves.

Dazed but curious, Emma began to explore. She wandered through the crowded streets, marvelling at the grandeur of St. Paul's Cathedral, the beauty of the Thames River, and the imposing presence of the Tower of London. Everything felt incredibly real—the scent of fresh bread from a nearby bakery, the chill of the river breeze, the texture of the cobblestones under her feet.

Emma's journey through London felt like a dream. She visited the British Museum, where ancient artifacts told stories of long-forgotten civilizations. She strolled through Hyde Park, where children played and artists captured the landscape on their canvases. At Covent Garden, she watched street performers and listened to musicians fill the air with melodies.

As the days passed, Emma found herself falling in love with London. She made friends with a kind bookseller named Thomas, who ran a quaint little shop near Piccadilly Circus. Thomas was fascinated by Emma's tales of modern life and her mysterious arrival. Together, they explored the city's hidden gems, from the secret gardens of Kensington to the bustling markets of Camden.

One evening, as they sat by the fire in Thomas's shop, Emma confided in him about the enchanted book. Thomas listened intently, his eyes widening with amazement. "Perhaps the book is waiting for you to fulfill a purpose here," he suggested. "Maybe it brought you here for a reason."

Intrigued by the idea, Emma pondered what her purpose might be. She decided to help Thomas save his struggling bookshop by organising a grand literary festival. They invited authors, poets, and artists from all over London, and the event was a resounding success. The shop thrived, becoming a beloved cultural hub.

On the final night of the festival, as Emma and Thomas celebrated their triumph, she felt the familiar pull of the book once more. She knew it was time to return home. With a heavy heart, she said her goodbyes, promising to never forget the magical city and the friends she had made.

Emma awoke in her reading chair, the book still open in her lap. She glanced around, half-expecting to see London outside her window. The rain had stopped, and the room was filled with the golden light of the setting sun. She closed the book, a wistful smile on her lips.

The experience had felt so real, yet she knew it was a journey of the heart and mind. Emma visited Mr. Whitaker the next day and recounted her adventure. He listened with a knowing smile and a twinkle in his eye. "Books have a magic all their own," he said. "They can take us places we never imagined."

From that day on, Emma cherished "The Enchanted Traveler: A Guide to London" as her most prized possession. She often revisited its pages, each time feeling a hint of the magic she had once experienced. And though she never physically returned to London, the city remained alive in her heart, a testament to the power of imagination and the enduring enchantment of books.

Welcome to London, a city where history, culture, and advancement crash in a stunning showcase of metropolitan loftiness. From its old Roman roots to its status as a worldwide force to be reckoned with, London offers an exceptional mix of the old and the new, the conventional and the cutting edge. Whether you're a first-time guest or a carefully prepared explorer, this guide will assist you with exploring the city's notable tourist spots, unlikely treasures, and in the middle between.

London is a city of neighborhoods, each with its own unmistakable person and appeal. Walk around the cobblestone roads of Covent Nursery, where road entertainers and store shops make a lively air. Meander the notable rear entryways of the East End, rich with stories of Jack the Ripper and the origin of the advanced trendy person scene. Cross the grand Pinnacle Scaffold to find the South

Bank's creative style and the clamouring markets of Precinct.

The city's horizon is a demonstration of its celebrated past and aggressive future. From the middle age magnificence of the Pinnacle of London to the cutting edge outline of The Shard, each side of London recounts a story. Visit the fantastic corridors of the English Exhibition hall and wonder about treasures from across the globe, or lose yourself in the contemporary magnum opuses at the Tate Current. What's more, no outing to London is finished without a photograph operation at Buckingham Castle, where you could get a brief look at the Top-down reorganizing.

Yet, London is something beyond its tourist spots. It's a city of encounters. Appreciate the culinary pleasures of its different food scene, from Michelin-featured eateries to comfortable bars serving conventional fried fish and French fries. Partake in a night out in the West End, home to elite theater creations and melodic party. Or on the other hand just loosen up in one of the city's many stops and gardens, as Hyde Park or Kew Nurseries, where nature gives a serene getaway from the metropolitan hustle.

Transportation in London is just about as unique as the actual city. The notorious red multi level buses, the effective Cylinder organization, and the beautiful Thames Waterway travels guarantee that getting around is basically as invigorating as the actual locations. What's more, with London's broad vehicle interfaces, the city's numerous attractions are generally inside simple reach.

This guide will be your friend as you investigate the profundities of London, offering insider tips, must-see spots, and pragmatic counsel to make your excursion extraordinary. Thus, gather your packs, get your Shellfish card, and prepare to set out on an undertaking through one of the world's most spellbinding urban areas. Welcome to London your remarkable excursion begins here.

Welcome to London

Welcome to London, a city where history and innovation entwine consistently, offering an encounter that is both spellbinding and different. As the capital of the Unified Realm, London is a worldwide city that draws in great many guests every year, drawn by its rich legacy, social liveliness, and vast open doors for investigation. Whether you're a set of experiences buff, a culture fan, or an admirer of the metropolitan way of life, London brings something to the table for everybody. We should leave on an excursion through this momentous city, finding its famous tourist spots, social fortunes, and extraordinary person.

A Verifiable Embroidery

London's set of experiences extends back north of two centuries, a course of events that is clearly reflected in its design, exhibition halls, and streetscapes. The city was established by the Romans as Londinium in Promotion 43, and leftovers of this antiquated past can in any case be seen today, for example, the remains of the Roman Wall close to Pinnacle Slope. The Pinnacle of London, an UNESCO World Legacy site, remains as an imposing image of the city's middle age history. Initially worked by William the Champion in 1078, the Pinnacle has filled in as a regal castle, jail, and depository, and presently houses the Royal gems.

A walk around the Thames Stream uncovers a scene of London's development. The glorious Places of Parliament and the notable Enormous Ben are demonstration of the city's political legacy, while the close by Westminster Monastery has seen hundreds of years of crowning celebrations, weddings, and burial services of English rulers. Crossing the waterway, the South Bank offers a juxtaposition of old and new, from the notable Globe Theater, a dedicated reproduction of Shakespeare's unique playhouse, to the cutting edge wonder of the London Eye, giving stunning perspectives on the city's horizon.

Social Kaleidoscope

London is a social mosaic, where various impacts join to make a lively and dynamic environment. The English Historical centre, with its tremendous assortment traversing centuries and landmasses, is a demonstration of the city's job as a worldwide social centre point. Guests can wonder about the Rosetta Stone, the Elgin Marbles, and the Egyptian mummies, all under one rooftop. The Public Exhibition and the Tate Present day feature works of art of old style and contemporary workmanship, offering something for each imaginative taste.

The West End, London's auditorium region, rivals Broadway with its astonishing cluster of creations. From immortal works of art like "Les Misérables" and "The Ghost of the Drama" to imaginative new works, the phases of London offer elite exhibitions that charm crowds a large number of evenings. For music darlings, the city is a shelter, with settings like the Imperial Albert Corridor, the O2 Field, and endless cozy clubs facilitating exhibitions going from traditional ensembles to state of the art rock and pop.

A Culinary Experience

London's culinary scene is essentially as different as its populace, offering a worldwide gastronomic experience that takes care of all palates. Customary English passage, like fried fish and French fries, broil meals, and evening tea, can be enjoyed in notable bars and rich lunch nooks. Precinct Market, one of the city's most established and biggest food markets, is a heaven for foodies, with its variety of high quality cheeses, new produce, and worldwide luxuries.

The city's multiculturalism is reflected in its culinary contributions. Block Path is renowned for its energetic Bangladeshi people group and delicious curry houses, while Chinatown close to Leicester Square is a clamouring territory of Asian eateries and shops. Whether you're in the mind-set for

Italian pasta, Center Eastern mezze, or Japanese sushi, London's areas offer a culinary excursion all over the planet.

Green Spaces and Metropolitan Desert gardens

Regardless of its clamouring metropolitan climate, London is home to an overflow of green spaces and stops that give a serene break from the city's hurrying around. Hyde Park, one of the biggest and most renowned parks, offers huge open spaces, tranquil lakes, and the notable Speaker's Corner. Official's Park is eminent for its flawlessly finished gardens, sailing lake, and the a-list ZSL London Zoo.

For a more private encounter, the enchanting squares and gardens of Bloomsbury give a quiet retreat, while Hampstead Heath offers tough normal excellence and all encompassing perspectives on the city from Parliament Slope. The Regal Botanic Nurseries at Kew, an UNESCO World Legacy site, brags one the most different assortments of plants on the planet, set inside staggering scenes that change with the seasons.

A Cutting edge City

London isn't just a city saturated with history and culture yet additionally a flourishing current city. The monetary region, with its transcending high rises like The Shard and the Gherkin, represents the city's job as a worldwide financial force to be reckoned with. The shopping locale of Oxford Road, Official Road, and Covent Nursery are a customer's heaven, offering all that from top of the line design to peculiar stores.

The city's vehicle framework, including the famous red multi level buses and the broad Underground organisation, makes exploring London advantageous and effective. Every area has its own special person, from the hip and stylish energies of Shoreditch and Camden to the exquisite complexity of Chelsea and Kensington.

Why Visit London?

London, a city where history and advancement exist together in a stunning mix, is an objective that catches the hearts of millions every year. From its notable milestones and rich social legacy to its energetic expressions scene and culinary pleasures, London offers an unrivaled encounter for voyagers, all things considered. This paper investigates why London ought to be at the highest point of your movement list.

A Stroll Through History

London's authentic importance is irrefutable. The city is a residing exhibition hall, with destinations like the Pinnacle of London, Westminster Convent, and the Places of Parliament recounting the narrative of a country that has molded world history. The Pinnacle of London, an image of

Norman triumph, plays served different parts from an imperial royal residence to a jail, lodging the Royal gems that actually stun guests today. Westminster Nunnery, the crowning celebration church starting around 1066, isn't just a structural wonder yet in addition a resting place for eminent figures like Sir Isaac Newton and Charles Dickens.

For those entranced by illustrious history, Buckingham Castle offers a brief look into the existence of the English government. The Top-down reorganising function is a priority exhibition of English display. Also, the English Historical center houses a broad assortment of relics, including the Rosetta Stone and the Elgin Marbles, giving knowledge into old developments and their associations with current London.

A Social Kaleidoscope

London's social variety is perhaps of its most prominent strength. The city is a blend where north of 300 dialects are spoken, making an exceptional embroidery of customs and customs. This variety is reflected in its celebrations, markets, and neighbourhoods. Regions like Block Path, with its dynamic Bangladeshi people group, and Chinatown, overflowing with Asian cooking and culture, exhibit the city's multicultural substance.

Human expressions flourish in London, home to widely acclaimed foundations like the Public Exhibition, the Tate Current, and the Illustrious Show House. The West End theater region equals New York's Broadway, offering a variety of exhibitions from exemplary Shakespearean plays at the Globe Theater to state of the art creations. Music sweethearts can enjoy the rich embroidered artwork of sounds at settings like the Imperial Albert Lobby and the O2 Field, where top global specialists perform routinely.

Culinary Undertakings

London's food scene is essentially as different as its populace. From customary English admission like fried fish and French fries and Sunday dishes to worldwide cooking styles that mirror the city's worldwide impact, there is something to fulfill each sense of taste. District Market, one of London's most established and biggest food markets, offers a cornucopia of new produce, distinctive cheeses, and connoisseur road food. Michelin-featured cafés like The Ledbury and Sketch give a top notch food experience, while food trucks and spring up restaurants offer inventive and reasonable choices.

Evening tea is a quintessentially English encounter that ought not be missed. Famous foundations like The Ritz and Fortnum and Bricklayer serve this superb custom with polish, offering a choice of finely blended teas, sensitive finger sandwiches, and luscious cakes.

Green Spaces and Picturesque Excellence

Notwithstanding its clamoring metropolitan climate, London brags an overflow green spaces that offer serenity and regular magnificence. Hyde Park, one of the city's biggest parks, furnishes a quiet departure with its sailing lake, rose nursery, and outdoors occasions. Official's Park, home to the famous London Zoo, highlights lovely nurseries and a beautiful drifting lake. For all encompassing perspectives on the city, a visit to Primrose Slope or the Sky Nursery is strongly suggested.

The Thames Waterway, twisting through the core of London, adds to the city's appeal. A waterway journey offers a remarkable point of view of milestones, for example, the Pinnacle Scaffold, the London Eye, and the Shard, mixing old and new in a staggering visual presentation.

Shopping and Advancement

London is a customer's heaven, taking care of all preferences and financial plans. Oxford Road and Official Road are fixed with lead stores of global brands, while Bond Road offers extravagance shopping at planner shops. For an interesting shopping experience, visit Covent Nursery and Camden Market, where you can find everything from high quality specialties to rare design.

Advancement is at the center of London's personality. The city is a worldwide center for money, innovation, and inventive ventures. Regions like Silicon Indirect in Shoreditch have become inseparable from tech new companies and development. The Science Gallery and the Regular History Historical center give intelligent displays that rouse interest and learning for all ages.

How to Use This Guide

Leaving on another excursion, whether it's a task, a learning try, or an undertaking, requires the right devices and a reasonable arrangement. This guide is intended to be your confided in friend, giving you fundamental bits of knowledge, pragmatic exhortation, and significant stages to guarantee your prosperity. This is the way to take advantage of this aide.

Figuring out the Construction

To explore this guide really, understanding its structure is fundamental. The aide is coordinated into clear segments, each zeroing in on a particular part of your excursion. These segments are intended to be both exhaustive and succinct, permitting you to find the data you really want rapidly and without any problem.

1. **Introduction**: Gives an outline of the aide's inspiration and what you can hope to acquire from it.

2. **Step-by-Step** Guidelines: Itemised directions to assist you with achieving explicit assignments or objectives.

3. **Tips and Best Practices**: Master counsel and techniques to advance your endeavors and stay away from normal entanglements.

4. **Resources**: An organised rundown of extra materials, like books, sites, and instruments, to additional help your excursion.

5. **FAQs**: Replies to normal inquiries that might emerge as you explore through the aide.

6.   Summary and Subsequent stages: A compact recap of central issues and ideas for what to do straightaway.

Beginning

Start by perusing the prologue to figure out the extension and goals of the aide. This will furnish you with a reasonable thought of how the aide can assist you with accomplishing your objectives. Really focus on any requirements or suggested arrangements framed in this segment.

Following the Means

Each bit by bit guidance is intended to be not difficult to follow, with clear and brief language. This is the way to move toward them:

•   Peruse Completely: Take as much time as is needed to painstakingly peruse each step. Try not to rush, as missing subtleties can prompt false impressions.

• Follow Successively: The means are introduced in a consistent request, expanding on one another. Guarantee you follow them successively to stay away from disarray.

• Take Notes: Scribble down central issues, experiences, or any inquiries that emerge as you go through the means. This will assist with building up your comprehension and act as a source of perspective.

Using Tips and Best Practices

The tips and best practices area is loaded with master bits of knowledge to improve your excursion. This is the way to take full advantage of it:

• Apply Relevantly: Not all tips might apply straightforwardly to your particular circumstance. Utilize your judgment to figure out which guidance is generally pertinent.

• Explore and Adjust: Go ahead and try different things with various procedures. What works best can fluctuate from one individual to another, so adjust the tips to accommodate your extraordinary conditions.

• Reflect and Move along: Consistently ponder what you've realized and how you've applied it. Nonstop improvement is critical to long haul achievement.

Investigating Extra Assets

The assets segment gives an abundance of extra data to extend your insight and abilities. This is the way to use these assets:

• Focus on: Begin with the most pertinent assets that line up with your nearby necessities or interests.

• Broaden: Investigate a blend of various sorts of assets, like books, articles, recordings, and online courses, to acquire a balanced comprehension.

• Lock in: Effectively draw in with the material by taking notes, examining with friends, or in any event, contacting creators or specialists for additional bits of knowledge.

Resolving Normal Inquiries

The FAQ segment is an important asset for tending to any vulnerabilities or difficulties you could experience. This is the way to successfully utilize it:

• Audit In advance: Skim through the FAQs prior to plunging into the principal content to find out about likely difficulties and their answers.
• Allude Back: When you experience a particular issue, allude back to the FAQs for speedy responses and investigating tips.
• Contribute: In the event that you have questions not canvassed in the FAQ, think about searching out replies from applicable networks or specialists, and offer your discoveries to help other people.

Recapping and Pushing Ahead

The outline and following stages area is intended to support your learning and give clear heading to what to do straightaway. This is the way to utilize it:

• Audit Central issues: Go over the synopsis to guarantee you've embraced the primary ideas and steps.

• Plan Your Following stages: In light of the following stages gave, make a substantial strategy. Put forth attainable objectives and courses of events to keep up with energy.

• Remain Committed: Continue to return to the aide depending on the situation to keep focused and learn.

Chapter 1:. Planning Your Trip

Arranging an outing can be one of the most invigorating yet overwhelming undertakings for any voyager. From choosing an objective to booking facilities and making a schedule, the interaction requires cautious thought and association. This exposition gives an extensive manual for arranging your ideal outing, guaranteeing that everything about covered for a smooth and pleasant get-away.

Picking Your Objective

The most vital phase in arranging an outing is choosing the objective. Consider your inclinations and what you desire to acquire from your movements. Could it be said that you are looking for unwinding on a tropical ocean side, a gutsy trip across mountains, a social investigation of old urban communities, or a culinary excursion through connoisseur objections? Research potential areas that match your inclinations and fit affordable enough for you.

While settling on an objective, require into account the season you intend to travel. A few spots are best visited during explicit seasons to keep away from outrageous weather patterns or pinnacle vacationer swarms. For instance, visiting Europe throughout the mid year can be magnificent, however winter offers an alternate, frequently less jam-packed insight with happy business sectors and snow-covered scenes.

Setting a Financial plan

Laying out a spending plan is urgent in guaranteeing your excursion is monetarily doable. Think about every single likely cost, including transportation, convenience, food, exercises, and keepsakes. It's crucial for represent both fixed costs (like flights and inn appointments) and variable expenses (like everyday dinners and exercises).

To set aside cash, search for arrangements and limits. Sites and applications that think about flight and lodging costs can assist you with tracking down the best arrangements. Consider going during the off-top season when costs are ordinarily lower, and search for comprehensive bundles that group flights, facilities, and once in a while even exercises at a decreased rate.

Booking Flights and Convenience

Whenever you've picked your objective and set a spending plan, now is the right time to book your flights and convenience. Begin by exploring flight choices to track down the most helpful and reasonable courses. Consider factors, for example, delay times, carrier surveys, and extra expenses for things.

While choosing convenience, contemplate your inclinations and requirements. Do you favor the advantage of a lodging, the warm feel of a get-away rental, or the social climate of an inn? Understand surveys, look at costs, and check the area's vicinity to the attractions you intend to visit. Booking ahead of time frequently gets better rates and more choices.

Making a Schedule

A very much arranged schedule guarantees you capitalise on your time at your objective. Begin by posting the priority attractions and exercises, then bunch them by area to limit travel time. Be practical about what you can accomplish in a day and consider some adaptability. Over-planning can prompt burnout, while under-booking can leave you with inactive time.

Research neighbourhood customs, occasions, and opening times to stay away from shocks. A few attractions might require early bookings, so plan in like manner. Consolidate time for unwinding and unconstrained investigation to partake in the embodiment of your objective really.

Getting ready for the Excursion

Readiness is critical to a smooth outing. Make an agenda of fundamentals to pack, taking into account the environment and exercises arranged. Significant things incorporate travel reports (identification, visas, tickets), prescriptions, travel protection, and an emergency treatment pack. Pack adaptable attire that can be layered and blend-and-coordinated.

Guarantee your monetary game plans are all together. Educate your bank regarding your itinerary items to keep away from any issues with card exchanges abroad. Convey a blend of instalment techniques, including cash, Visas, and a movement card for crises.

Exploring Transportation

Understanding neighbourhood transportation choices can incredibly upgrade your movement experience. Research the most ideal ways to get around, whether it's public travel, taxis, rental vehicles, or rideshare administrations. Numerous urban communities offer travel passes that give limitless admittance to public vehicle at a proper value, which can be both helpful and conservative.

Consider downloading disconnected guides and transportation applications to explore without requiring steady web access. Really get to know the nearby traffic rules on the off chance that you intend to lease a vehicle.

Remaining Protected and Solid

Security and wellbeing are vital while voyaging. Research any tourism warnings or security worries for your objective. Keep your possessions secure and know about your environmental elements, particularly in jam-packed vacationer regions. It's fitting to have duplicates of significant archives and crisis contacts saved carefully and on paper.

Remain sound by drinking packaged or sifted water on the off chance that neighborhood regular water isn't protected, and be wary of road food assuming you have a touchy stomach. Travel protection that covers health related crises can give inner harmony.

Embracing the Experience

At long last, recall that movement is about the experience. Embrace the way of life, attempt new food sources, get familiar with a couple of expressions in the neighbourhood language, and draw in with local people. Be available to surprising undertakings and changes in plans. The best travel recollections frequently come from impromptu minutes and unconstrained choices.

Best Time to Visit

Picking the best opportunity to visit London can be trying because of the city's allure consistently. Each season offers an exceptional viewpoint on this powerful city, from its verifiable milestones and social merriments to its consistently evolving climate. This exposition gives a far-reaching manual for the best times to encounter London, considering the environment, occasions, and the general guest experience.

Spring: A Blooming Wonder (Walk to May)

Spring in London is a period of reestablishment and liveliness. As the city stirs from its colder time of year sleep, stops and gardens burst into sprout with daffodils, tulips, and cherry blooms, making it one of the most beautiful times to visit. The temperatures during this season are gentle, going from 8°C (46°F) to 15°C (59°F), establishing a wonderful climate for outside exercises.

Key occasions during spring incorporate the well known Chelsea Bloom Show in May, which exhibits shocking plant shows from around the world. Moreover, the London Long distance race draws in sprinters and onlookers from across the globe, adding a merry environment to the city. The boat race among Oxford and Cambridge colleges on the Thames is another feature, joining sports with custom.

Summer: Energetic and Merry (June to August)

Summer is seemingly the most well known chance to visit London, with warm temperatures averaging between 14°C (57°F) and 23°C (73°F). The long sunshine hours consider broadened touring, and the city is bursting at the seams with celebrations, open air occasions, and a clamoring air.

The English Mid year Hyde Park live concert draws significant worldwide specialists, while the Notting Slope Festival in August observes Caribbean culture with exuberant motorcades, music, and road food. Wimbledon, the world's most established tennis competition, happens in late June and early July, offering a quintessentially English encounter.

London's many parks, like Hyde Park, Official's Park, and Hampstead Heath, become ideal spots for picnics, sailing, and outdoors shows. Outside theaters, for example, the Official's Park Outdoors Theater, give a remarkable method for getting a charge out of exemplary plays under the stars.

Pre-winter: A Brilliant Change (September to November)

Pre-winter in London is a time of dazzling varieties and agreeable climate, with temperatures going from 9°C (48°F) to 18°C (64°F). The city's parks and roads are enhanced with brilliant leaves, making a beautiful scenery for investigating.

September and October are ideal months to encounter London's social contributions without the pinnacle summer swarms. The Absolutely Thames celebration praises the waterway with craftsmanship establishments, exhibitions, and directed strolls. The BFI London Film Celebration in October grandstands the best in worldwide film, drawing in film aficionados and VIPs the same.

November brings the Master City chairman's Show, a memorable parade tracing all the way back to the thirteenth hundred years, highlighting floats, music, and firecrackers. Huge fire Night on November fifth lights up the skies with firecrackers, recognizing the bombed Explosive Plot of 1605.

Winter: Happy and Comfortable (December to February)

Winter in London is a mystical time, particularly during the Christmas season. Temperatures range from 2°C (36°F) to 8°C (46°F), and keeping in mind that it seldom snows, the city embraces the merry soul with stunning lights and improvements.

The Christmas time frame sees notable spots like Covent Nursery, Official Road, and Oxford Road changed into winter wonderlands. Ice skating arenas spring up at the Regular History Exhibition hall, Somerset House, and the Pinnacle of London, offering fun exercises in shocking settings. Winter Wonderland in Hyde Park is a must-visit, with its bubbly market, carnival rides, and ice models.

January and February are calmer months, making it a brilliant opportunity to investigate exhibition halls and displays without the groups. The New Year's

Day March is an energetic method for starting off the year, while Chinese New Year festivities in Chinatown offer a vivacious social encounter.

Budgeting Your Trip

London, prestigious for its rich history, energetic culture, and different attractions, is a fantasy objective for some voyagers. Notwithstanding, it's additionally known for being one of the more costly urban areas on the planet. Dread not — this guide will tell you the best way to financially plan your excursion to London, guaranteeing you experience the best of what the city brings to the table without burning through every last dollar.

Preparing: Exploration and Booking

The initial step to a spending plan cordial excursion to London is exhaustive preparation and early reserving. Flights can be quite possibly of the main cost, however reserving a while ahead of time can yield significant investment funds. Go through admission correlation sites and set value alarms to track down the best arrangements. Consider flying into elective air terminals like Gatwick or Stansted, which frequently have less expensive flights contrasted with Heathrow.

For convenience, investigate spending plan inns, lodgings, or get-away rentals. Sites like Airbnb, Booking.com, and Hostelworld offer different choices that can suit various spending plans. Remaining in regions somewhat outside the downtown area, like Camden, Hackney, or Hammersmith, can likewise set aside cash while as yet giving great admittance to public transportation.

Getting Around: Public Vehicle and Passes

London's public vehicle framework is productive and extensive, making it simple to get around without requiring a vehicle. The famous red transports and the broad Underground (Cylinder) network are practical ways of investigating the city. Buy a Clam card or utilize a contactless installment card to profit from limited passages and everyday covers.

For sightseers, the London Pass offers critical investment funds on section charges to many top attractions, including the Pinnacle of London, The Shard, and a bounce on-jump off transport visit. The Travelcard choice remembered for some London Pass bundles covers public vehicle inside assigned zones, offering amazing benefit for cash.

Free and Minimal expense Attractions

London is home to various free attractions that can make your outing both charming and reasonable. Numerous top notch exhibition halls and displays, like the English Historical headquarters, the Public Display, the Tate Current, and the Regular History Gallery, offer free passage. These foundations give long periods of diversion and training at no expense.

Investigate the city's delightful parks, like Hyde Park, Official's Park, and Greenwich Park, which offer beautiful strolling ways, gardens, and, surprisingly, free occasions. Walk around the South Bank of the Thames for shocking perspectives on milestones like the London Eye and Pinnacle Scaffold. Try not to miss the Top-down restructuring function at Buckingham Royal residence, another free display that features English practice.

Reasonable Feasting Choices

London's culinary scene is assorted and takes care of all financial plans. For a sample of neighborhood culture without the excessive cost tag, visit road food markets, for example, District Market, Camden Market, and Portobello Street Market. These business sectors offer a great many reasonable and tasty choices from around the world.

For a formal dinner, search out spending plan well disposed chain eateries like Wetherspoons, Pret A Trough, and Itsu. Numerous bars offer generous feasts at sensible costs, particularly during noon. Exploit pre-theater menus and offers for early risers at cafés in the West End.

Supermarkets as sainsbury Tesco's, and Lidl give reasonable choices to the people who like to set up their own feasts. Consider picnicking in one of London's many parks for a charming and cheap feasting experience.

Shrewd Shopping and Amusement

London is a customer's heaven, yet it's not difficult to overspend if you don't watch out. For one of a kind and spending plan well disposed finds, investigate rare shops, secondhand shops, and markets like Spitalfields and Block Path. These

48

spots offer unique things at costs that won't burn through every last cent.

Amusement in London doesn't need to be costly. Search for limited performance center tickets at the TKTS stall in Leicester Square or on sites like TodayTix. Numerous historical centers and displays have free occasions, talks, and presentations, giving social encounters at no expense. Also, London's dynamic music scene incorporates free gigs and open mic evenings at different bars and settings across the city.

Extra Tips and Deceives

• **Travel Protection**: Consistently put resources into venture out protection to safeguard yourself against unexpected costs like health related crises or excursion abrogations.
• **Cash Trade**: Try not to trade cash at air terminals or traveller areas of interest. Use ATMs or cash trade administrations with serious rates to get more incentive for your cash.

- **Remain Associated**: Consider buying a nearby SIM card or a versatile Wi-Fi gadget to try not to high wander charges. Numerous bistros, eateries, and public regions offer free Wi-Fi.

Travel Insurance

Travelling to London is an exciting prospect, filled with the promise of exploring historic landmarks, vibrant cultural scenes, and world-class dining. However, alongside the excitement, it's essential to consider practicalities such as travel insurance. Travel insurance might seem like just another expense, but it is a crucial investment that can protect you from unforeseen circumstances and provide peace of mind. This essay delves into why travel insurance is essential for your trip to London, what it typically covers, and how to choose the right policy.

Why You Need Travel Insurance for London

London, like any major city, comes with its share of unpredictable situations that can disrupt your travel plans. Travel insurance offers a safety net against various potential issues, ensuring that your trip remains as stress-free and enjoyable as possible.

1. Medical Emergencies: While the United Kingdom has a robust healthcare system, medical treatment for non-residents can be expensive. Travel insurance typically covers medical expenses incurred during your trip, from minor illnesses to more serious injuries. This coverage is crucial as it can save you from exorbitant medical bills and provide access to necessary treatments without financial strain.

2. Trip Cancellations and Interruptions: Unforeseen events such as personal emergencies, natural disasters, or even global health crises can lead to trip cancellations or interruptions. Travel insurance can reimburse non-refundable expenses such as flights, accommodations, and tour bookings, ensuring you don't lose money if your plans change unexpectedly.

3. **Lost or Delayed Baggage:** Airlines occasionally misplace or delay baggage, which can be particularly inconvenient if you're in a foreign country. Travel insurance policies often include coverage for lost, stolen, or delayed luggage, allowing you to replace essential items and continue your trip without significant disruption.

4. **Travel Delays:** Flights can be delayed or cancelled due to various reasons, including weather conditions, technical issues, or strikes. Travel insurance can cover additional accommodation, meals, and transportation costs incurred due to these delays, helping you manage unexpected expenses and maintain your travel plans.

5. **Personal Liability:** Accidents can happen anywhere, and if you accidentally cause damage to property or injury to someone else, you could be held legally responsible. Travel insurance often includes personal liability coverage, protecting you from potentially significant financial liability.

What Travel Insurance Typically Covers

While specific coverage details can vary between policies, most comprehensive travel insurance plans include the following:

- **Medical Coverage:** Emergency medical treatment, hospitalizations, and sometimes dental emergencies.
- **Trip Cancellation/Interruption:** Reimbursement for non-refundable travel expenses if your trip is cancelled or interrupted due to covered reasons.
- **Baggage and Personal Belongings:** Compensation for lost, stolen, or damaged luggage and personal items.
- **Travel Delay:** Coverage for additional expenses incurred due to flight or other travel delays.
- **Emergency Evacuation:** Costs associated with emergency medical evacuation or repatriation to your home country.
- **Accidental Death and Dismemberment:** Benefits paid to beneficiaries in

the event of accidental death or serious injury while touring.

• **24/7 Assistance Services:** Access to travel assistance services for help with medical emergencies, legal issues, or travel arrangements.

How to Choose the Right Travel Insurance Policy

Selecting the right travel insurance policy requires careful consideration of your travel needs and the specifics of your trip to London. Here are some tips to help you choose wisely:

1. **Assess Your Needs:** Consider factors such as the duration of your trip, planned activities, and any pre-existing medical conditions. Ensure the policy you choose covers all potential risks specific to your trip.
2. **Compare Policies:** Don't settle for the first policy you come across. Compare different providers and their offerings to find a policy that provides comprehensive coverage at a reasonable price.

3. **Read the Fine Print:** Understand the policy's exclusions and limitations. For instance, some policies may not cover certain adventure activities or pre-existing medical conditions without additional coverage.

4. **Check the Provider's Reputation:** Research the insurance company's reputation, customer reviews, and claims process. A provider with a good track record of customer service and efficient claims handling is preferable.

5. **Consider Additional Coverage:** Depending on your specific needs, you might require additional coverage such as rental car insurance, high-value item coverage, or extended medical coverage.

Essential Travel Apps

Making a trip to London can be an exhilarating encounter, with its rich history, dynamic culture, and clamoring roads. To capitalize on your visit, having the right travel applications on your cell phone can be a distinct advantage. These applications can assist you with exploring the city, track down the best places to eat, and find unexpected, yet invaluable treasures. Here is an exhaustive manual for the fundamental travel applications you'll require for an extraordinary London experience.

Citymapper: Dominating London's Vehicle Framework

Citymapper is a basic application for exploring London's perplexing transportation organization. Whether you're utilizing the Cylinder, transports, cable cars, or bicycles, Citymapper gives continuous data on courses, timetables, and disturbances. Its easy to use interface makes it simple to design your excursion, offering various choices to get from point A to point B, including strolling and cycling courses. The application additionally gives refreshes on postponements and elective courses, guaranteeing you get to your objective effectively.

TfL Shellfish and Contactless: Working on Your Drive

Transport for London's (TfL) Clam and Contactless application is an unquestionable requirement for dealing with your movement installments. This application permits you to top up your Shellfish card, view your excursion history, and track your spending. It additionally upholds contactless installment strategies, making it simpler to jump on and off open vehicle without agonizing over paper tickets. With this application, you can consistently coordinate your movement spending plan and keep away from the problem of ticket lines.

Google Guides: Your Definitive Route Device

Google Guides is a staple for any explorer. In London, it's especially valuable for finding the best courses, whether you're strolling, driving, or utilizing public vehicle. The application gives itemized maps, road perspectives, and constant traffic refreshes. It additionally features close by attractions, cafés, and shops, permitting you to find nearby top choices and vacationer areas of interest the same. With disconnected map capacities, you can explore the city even without a web association.

Uber: Advantageous and Solid Rides

While London's dark taxis are notorious, Uber offers a helpful option for getting around the city. The Uber application permits you to book rides effortlessly, view assessed passages, and track your driver's appearance. With different ride choices accessible, from spending plan well disposed UberX to sumptuous UberLUX, you can pick a help that meets your requirements and spending plan. The application likewise gives wellbeing highlights, including driver evaluations and outing sharing choices, guaranteeing a solid ride.

TripAdvisor: Find the Best of London

TripAdvisor is a fundamental application for tracking down first class attractions, eateries, and exercises in London. With a large number of surveys from voyagers all over the planet, you can settle on informed conclusions about where to go and what to do. The application's "Close by" include assists you with tracking down focal points inside your area, while its "What should be done" segment features famous visits and encounters. Client created content, including photographs and definite surveys, offers bona fide bits of knowledge into every area.

OpenTable: Consistent Eating Reservations

London's culinary scene is different and dynamic, with endless eating choices to investigate. OpenTable improves on the most common way of finding and booking cafés. The application permits you to look for diners by food, area, and value reach, and view continuous accessibility. With client surveys and evaluations, you can pick the best spots to fulfill your culinary desires. OpenTable likewise offers elite arrangements and advancements, guaranteeing you take advantage of your feasting experience.

Break London: Your Social Aide

Break London is the go-to application for finding the city's social and diversion contributions. It gives state-of-the-art data on occasions, displays, shows, and theater exhibitions. The application's organized records, for example, "Top 10 Activities This Week," assist you with remaining in the loop about the most recent happenings. Whether you're keen on craftsmanship, music, or nightlife, Break London guarantees you never pass up the city's dynamic scene.

XE Money: Bother Free Cash Transformation

Dealing with your spending plan while voyaging can be testing, particularly with fluctuating trade rates. XE Cash is a solid application for continuous money change, assisting you with monitoring your spending in English pounds. The application permits you to screen various monetary standards, view authentic graphs, and set rate cautions. With disconnected usefulness, you can get to trade rates without a web association, guaranteeing you generally get the best incentive for your cash.

London Official Aide: Insider Tips and Visits

The London Official Aide application, created by Visit London, offers complete data and insider tips for travelers. It highlights intelligent guides, recommended agendas, and insights concerning significant attractions. The application's "Close by" include assists you with finding focal points near your area, while its occasion schedule keeps you refreshed on what's going on around the city. With proposals from local people and specialists, this application is your computerized local escort to London's tricks of the trade.

Chapter 2 Getting to London

London, the clamouring capital of the Unified Realm, is a top-notch objective that draws in a huge number of guests every year. Whether you're going for business, relaxation, or study, getting to London is an experience in itself. This paper gives a point by point guide on the different ways of arriving at London, guaranteeing a smooth beginning to your excursion in this famous city.

Via Air: The Worldwide Entryway

London is served by six global air terminals, making it quite possibly the most available city on the planet. Every air terminal takes care of various necessities, from extravagant travel to spending plan agreeable choices.

Heathrow Air terminal (LHR): Found 15 miles west of focal London, Heathrow is the most active air terminal in the UK and the essential center for

English Aviation routes. It offers broad associations with objections around the world. The Heathrow Express train gives a quick, 15-minute excursion to Paddington Station, while the Piccadilly Line of the London Underground offers a more practical, though longer, course into the city.

Gatwick Air terminal (LGW): Arranged 30 miles south of London, Gatwick is the second-biggest air terminal serving a blend of full-administration and minimal expense transporters. The Gatwick Express offers an immediate train administration to Victoria Station in around 30 minutes. Thameslink and Southern trains additionally associate Gatwick to different pieces of London and then some.

Stansted Air terminal (STN): Found 40 miles upper east of London, Stansted is a center point for minimal expense carriers, including Ryanair. The Stansted Express gives an immediate train connect to Liverpool Road Station in roughly 45 minutes.

Luton Air terminal (LTN): Arranged 35 miles north of London, Luton additionally serves principally financial plan carriers. The Luton Air terminal Express train, joined with a van transport, interfaces voyagers to St. Pancras Global Station in around 30 minutes.

London City Air terminal (LCY): Found only 6 miles east of focal London, City Air terminal provides food principally to business voyagers and offers speedy admittance to the monetary areas. The Docklands Light Railroad (DLR) interfaces the air terminal to the London Underground organisation.

Southend Air terminal (SEN): Around 40 miles east of London, Southend fills in as one more choice for financial plan flights, especially to European objections. Trains from Southend Air terminal station arrive at Liverpool Road Station in around 50 minutes.

Via Train: Productive and Panoramic detours

London's rail associations are broad, making it effectively open from different pieces of the UK and Europe.

Homegrown Trains: Significant train stations like Lord's Cross, St. Pancras, Euston, Paddington, Victoria, and Waterloo connect London to urban areas across the UK. Fast administrations like the Incomparable Western Railroad, Virgin Trains, and the new Elizabeth Line (Crossrail) guarantee speedy and agreeable travel.

Worldwide Trains: The Eurostar administration from St. Pancras Global associates London to Paris, Brussels, Amsterdam, and other European urban areas. This rapid train offers a helpful and eco-accommodating option in contrast to flying, with the excursion from London to Paris requiring a little more than two hours.

By Street: Adaptable and Grand Excursions

Venturing out to London by street can be an agreeable and adaptable choice, particularly for those investigating the UK or Europe via vehicle or mentor.

Driving: London is very much associated by an organisation of motorways and significant streets. The M25 motorway encloses the city, connecting to the M1, M4, M11, and other key courses. Notwithstanding, be ready for gridlock and consider using park-and-ride offices on the edges to try not to drive in the downtown area.

Mentors: Significant distance mentors are a prudent and agreeable method for arriving at London. Public Express and Megabus work administrations from different UK and European urban areas to Victoria Mentor Station. Mentors offer conveniences like Wi-Fi, electrical plugs, and open to seating, making the excursion wonderful.

Via Ocean: An Exceptional Journey

For those looking for an exceptional travel insight, showing up in London via ocean offers a beautiful and comfortable excursion.

Voyage Ships: London's port offices can oblige journey ships, with the essential mooring point at Greenwich. From here, traveller can undoubtedly get to the city's attractions by means of the Docklands Light Railroad or Thames Trimmers waterway administrations.

Ships: Ships from mainland Europe show up at ports like Dover, Harwich, and Portsmouth. From these ports, explorers can get trains or mentors to London. The Channel Passage likewise offers a ship elective for those driving from France to the UK.

Entry Requirements

Venturing out to London, one of the world's most energetic and generally rich urban communities, requires grasping its entrance necessities. Whether you are visiting for the travel industry, business, study, or work, being very much informed about the fundamental documentation and guidelines is fundamental for a smooth excursion. This paper gives a nitty gritty aide on the section prerequisites to London, covering visas, customs guidelines, wellbeing precautionary measures, and travel tips.

Visa Necessities

The requirement for a visa to enter London (and the UK) relies upon your ethnicity, reason for visit, and span of stay. Here is a breakdown of the essential classes:

1. **Tourist Visas:**

- **Without visa Nations**: Residents of numerous nations, including the US, Canada, Australia, and EU part states, can enter the UK without a visa for short stays of as long as a half year. During this period, guests can participate in the travel industry, visit loved ones, and go to conferences.

- **Standard Guest Visa**: Nationals from nations not qualified without a visa section should apply for a Standard Guest Visa. This visa considers stays of as long as a half year and covers the travel industry, business exercises, and short courses. The application cycle includes finishing an internet based structure, paying an expense, and giving biometric data.

2. Work Visas:

- **Gifted Labourer Visa:** For those wanting to work in London, the Talented Specialist Visa is fundamental. Candidates should have a bid for employment from an authorized UK boss and meet explicit expertise and compensation edges.

- **Brief Specialist Visas:** Classes like the Impermanent Labourer - Imaginative and

Brandishing visa take care of transient work valuable open doors in unambiguous ventures.

3. **Student Visas:**

• **Understudy Visa:** For long haul studies, like college degrees, non-EU nationals need an Understudy Visa. Candidates should have a proposal from an authorised UK instructive foundation and exhibit adequate monetary assets.

• **Transient Review Visa:** For courses as long as a half year, or 11 months for English language courses, the Momentary Review Visa is required.

4. **Family Visas:**

• Those joining relatives in the UK might require a Family Visa. This classification covers mates, accomplices, kids, and guardians.

Customs Guidelines

After showing up in London, voyagers should explore customs guidelines, which shift in light of their nation of takeoff and the things they are bringing.

1. **Personal Assets:**
• Individual things for individual use, like apparel, cameras, and workstations, are by and large obligation free.
• There are limits on how much liquor, tobacco, and gifts that can be brought into the UK without paying obligation. For instance, voyagers from non-EU nations can raise to 1 litre of spirits, 200 cigarettes, and gifts worth up to £390 obligation free.

2. **Restricted and Restricted Things:**
• Certain things are confined or denied, including guns, unlawful medications, and imperilled creature items. Explorers ought to check the UK government's true rules for a total rundown.

Wellbeing Safeguards

Wellbeing guidelines and prerequisites for entering London can shift, particularly considering the Coronavirus pandemic. Here are key contemplations:

1. Vaccinations:

- At present, there are no compulsory immunizations expected for section into the UK from most nations. Nonetheless, explorers ought to guarantee they are fully informed regarding routine inoculations.

2. COVID-19 Measures:

- Section prerequisites connected with Coronavirus, for example, evidence of inoculation, negative experimental outcomes, and quarantine conventions, have advanced over the long haul. Checking the most recent government counsel prior to travelling is essential.

3. Travel Protection:

- While not required, travel protection is strongly suggested. It can cover health related crises, trip abrogations, and other unexpected occasions.

Travel Tips

To guarantee a smooth section into London, think about the accompanying tips:

1. **Documentation:**
• Keep every expected record, including your identification, visa (if pertinent), and travel schedule, effectively open. Guarantee your identification is legitimate for no less than a half year past your expected stay.
2. **Arrival Structure:**
• A few explorers might have to finish an arrival card or traveller finder structure before appearance. Check if this applies to your outing.

3. **Customs Statement:**
• Tell the truth and be clear while pronouncing things at customs. Inability to do so can bring about fines or seizure of products.
4. **Transport Choices:**
• Upon appearance, London offers different vehicle choices, including the Underground (Cylinder), transports, and cabs. The

Heathrow Express train gives a quick association from Heathrow Air terminal to focal London.

Chapter 3: Getting Around

London, with its rambling scene and heap attractions, can appear to be overwhelming to explore. Be that as it may, the city's exhaustive and effective vehicle framework makes getting around shockingly simple and pleasant. This exposition investigates the different methods of transportation accessible in London, giving experiences and tips to assist guests with capitalizing on their excursion through this lively city.

The London Underground: The Foundation of the City

The London Underground, regularly known as the Cylinder, is the most established and one of the most broad metro frameworks on the planet. With 11 lines and 270 stations, it associates basically every side of the city. The Cylinder is a fundamental method of transport for the two local people and vacationers, offering fast and helpful admittance to significant milestones and communities.

Key Ways to Utilize the Cylinder:

• **Clam Card or Contactless Instalment:** Buy a Shellfish Card or utilize a contactless charge/Mastercard for consistent travel. These choices are less expensive than purchasing single tickets and can be utilised across all open vehicle.

• **Top Hours:** Try not to go during top hours (7:30-9:30 AM and 5:00-7:00 PM) to get away from the rush and partake in a more agreeable ride.

• **Tube Guide:** Dive more deeply into the Cylinder map. Free guides are accessible at stations, and advanced forms can be downloaded to your cell phone.

Transports: Investigating the City Over the Ground

London's notorious red multi level buses offer a beautiful method for getting around the city. With more than 700 courses, the transport network arrives at regions not covered by the Cylinder, making it an incredible choice for complete investigation. Transports run 24 hours, with night transports covering significant courses after the Cylinder closes.

Key Ways to Utilise Transports:

• **Clam Card or Contactless Instalment:** Utilise similar instalment strategies as the Cylinder. Note that money isn't acknowledged on transports.

• **Transport Stops:** Transport stops show course maps and live appearance times. Use applications like Citymapper to design your excursion.

• **Touring:** Consider taking courses like the 9 or 15, which pass by prominent

77

milestones, for example, Trafalgar Square, the Pinnacle of London, and St. Paul's House of God.

The Docklands Light Railroad (DLR): Interfacing East London

The DLR serves the Docklands region and portions of East London, including Canary Wharf and Greenwich. It is completely robotized, offering a special driverless encounter. The DLR is particularly valuable for arriving at attractions like the Regal Observatory, the Cutty Sark, and the Succeed Presentation Center.

Key Ways to Utilise the DLR:

• Clam Card or Contactless Instalment: similar instalment strategies apply.
• **Front Seats:** For a tomfoolery experience, sit at the front for a driver's-eye perspective on the excursion.

Overground and Public Rail: Growing Your Viewpoints

The London Overground supplements the Cylinder by associating rural regions to the downtown area. Public Rail administrations connect London with different urban communities and towns across the UK, making it simple to require roadtrips to objections like Windsor, Oxford, and Brighton.

Key Ways to utilise Overground and Public Rail:

• Tickets: Utilise a Clam Card or buy tickets at stations. For longer excursions, book ahead of time to get the best passages.
• Stations: Significant stations like Ruler's Cross, Paddington, and Victoria are exceptional with conveniences and give admittance to various lines and administrations.

Cycling: An Eco-Accommodating Choice

Cycling is progressively well known in London, because of broad bicycle paths and the city's bicycle sharing plan, Santander Cycles. Leasing a bicycle is simple and reasonable, and it offers a sound and eco-accommodating method for investigating the city at your own speed.

Key Ways to cycle:

• Bicycle Sharing: Recruit a Santander Cycle from docking stations across the city. The initial 30 minutes of each ride are free, making it a financially savvy choice.
• Security: Wear a head protector, keep traffic guidelines, and use bicycle paths where accessible.
• Courses: Investigate tourist detours like the Thames Way or Official's Channel for a charming ride.

Strolling: Finding Unexpected, yet invaluable treasures

Strolling is one of the most incredible ways of encountering London's appeal and character. A significant number of the city's attractions are inside strolling distance of one another, and walking around its roads permits you to find unexpected, yet invaluable treasures and nearby joys.

Key Ways to walk:

• **Agreeable Shoes:** Wear agreeable footwear, as you'll probably make a great deal of progress.
• **Maps and Applications:** Use guides and route applications like Google Guides or Citymapper to find the best strolling courses.
• **Directed Visits:** Consider joining a mobile visit to find out about the city's set of experiences, design, and culture from learned guides.

Cabs and Ride-Sharing: Comfort At a higher cost than normal

For the people who favour house-to-house administration, London's dark taxis and ride-sharing administrations like Uber offer helpful yet pricier choices. Dark taxis are renowned for their educated drivers, who should pass the thorough "Information" test covering London's roads and milestones.

Key Tips for Cabs and Ride-Sharing:

• Admissions: Dark taxis use metres, and rates can be high, parti.
• Booking: Flag down dark taxis in the city or at assigned positions. Use applications to book ride-sharing administrations.
• Wellbeing: Guarantee the vehicle is ratified and the driver's ID is shown.

Public Transport

London's public vehicle framework is quite possibly of the most exhaustive and effective on the planet, consistently associating its rambling city. From the notorious red multi level buses to the broad Underground organisation, London offers a heap of choices for inhabitants and guests the same. This paper investigates the different methods of public vehicle accessible in London, featuring their elements, advantages, and ways to capitalize on your excursion.

The London Underground: The Foundation of the City

The London Underground, warmly known as the Cylinder, is the most seasoned and one of the most broad metro frameworks around the world. With 11 lines covering 270 stations, it fills in as the foundation of London's public vehicle. The Cylinder works from early morning until late around evening time, for certain lines offering 24-hour administration on ends of the week.

Exploring the Cylinder is generally direct, on account of the famous Cylinder map, variety coded lines, and successive assistance. Stations are very much signposted, and advanced shows give ongoing data. The Clam card and contactless instalment strategies offer advantageous and savvy ways of voyaging, with day to day and week after week covers guaranteeing you won't ever overpay.

Transports: The Notorious Red Two layers

London's red multi level buses are not only a method of transport; they are a social image. The transport network covers the whole city, arriving at regions that the Cylinder doesn't. Transports work every minute of every day, with night transports guaranteeing the network even after the Cylinder has shut.

Transport travel offers a novel point of view of the city, permitting you to see milestones and neighbourhoods from a higher place. Courses like the 11, which goes through Westminster and the City of London, give grand excursions for a portion of the expense of a direct visit. Constant updates are accessible at transport stops and on versatile applications, making it simple to design your excursion.

Docklands Light Rail line (DLR): Associating the East

The Docklands Light Rail line (DLR) serves the revived Docklands region, associating it with the remainder of London. The DLR works driverless trains, offering all encompassing perspectives on the city's advanced turns of events, including Canary Wharf and the Illustrious Docks. It's a fundamental connection for arriving at the Succeed London presentation focus and London City Air terminal.

The DLR incorporates flawlessly with the Cylinder and transport organisations, and a similar Shellfish card and contactless instalment choices apply. Stations are furnished with lifts and slopes, guaranteeing availability for all travellers.

Overground: Connecting Rural areas and Then some

The London Overground supplements the Cylinder and DLR, giving fundamental connections between rural regions and the downtown area. It interfaces a large number of objections, from the stylish neighbourhoods of Shoreditch and Hackney to the verdant rural areas of Richmond and Clapham.

Overground trains are present day and roomy, with clear signage and ordinary help. They offer an agreeable option in contrast to the Cylinder, particularly during top hours. The Overground network additionally incorporates the Elizabeth Line (previously Crossrail), which gives quick east-west associations across London and then some.

Cable cars: A South London Staple

Cable cars work in the south of London, essentially serving Croydon and encompassing regions. The cable car organisation, albeit restricted in scope, gives a proficient and dependable assistance for nearby suburbanites and guests.

Cable cars are open, with low floors and wide entryways, making them appropriate for travelers with portability issues. They offer a smooth and grand ride, interfacing key vehicle centres and shopping regions.

Stream Administrations: A Beautiful Other option

London's waterway administrations offer a grand and comfortable option in contrast to ordinary public vehicle. Waterway transports and ships work along the Thames, preventing at docks from Putney in the west to Woolwich in the east. Key objections incorporate Westminster, the South Bank, and Greenwich.

Waterway administrations give dazzling perspectives on London's horizon and milestones, for example, the Pinnacle Scaffold, the London Eye, and the Places of Parliament. They are an especially charming choice during a wonderful climate, consolidating transportation with touring.

Cycling and Strolling: Better Choices

London has taken critical steps in advancing cycling and strolling as reasonable vehicle choices. The city brags a broad organisation of cycle paths and bicycle sharing plans, like Santander Cycles, regularly known as "Boris Bicycles." Cycling offers an adaptable and harmless method for exploring London's roads and parks.

Strolling is one more brilliant method for investigating London, particularly in the downtown area where numerous attractions are inside a brief distance. The city's various pedestrianised regions and grand riverwalks go with strolling a pleasurable and viable decision.

Ways to involve Public Vehicle in London

1. Get a Clam Card: A Shellfish card or contactless instalment card is fundamental for helpful and financially savvy traversing all methods of public vehicles.
2. Plan Ahead: Use Transport for London (TfL) applications and sites to design your

excursion, check administration refreshes, and stay away from delays.

3. Travel Off-Pinnacle: Going beyond times of heavy traffic can assist you with staying away from swarmed conditions and partake in a more loosened up venture.

4. Mind the Hole: Focus on wellbeing declarations and signage, particularly on the Cylinder and at occupied stations.

5. Explore Elective Courses: London's public vehicle network offers different courses to most objections, so consider elective choices to stay away from clogs.

London Underground (Tube)

The London Underground, warmly known as the "Cylinder," is something beyond a transportation framework; it is a notable image of London itself. With its complex organisation of passages and stations, the Cylinder fills in as the soul of the city, consistently associating a huge number of travellers to their objections every day. This paper investigates the set of experiences, importance, and remarkable qualities of the London Underground, revealing insight into why it stays a wonder of metropolitan travel and a social insignia of London.

A Noteworthy Excursion

The London Underground holds the qualification of being the world's most memorable underground rail route. Its debut line, the Metropolitan Railroad, opened on January 10, 1863, running from Paddington to Farringdon. At first controlled by steam trains, the organization continuously extended and progressed to electric trains, altogether further developing proficiency and diminishing contamination.

The improvement of the Underground was driven by the need to lighten clog on London's roads. The development of profound level cylinder lines, beginning with the City and South London Rail line in 1890, considered greater and effective underground travel. The notable roundel logo and the particular Cylinder map, planned by Harry Beck in 1931, became persevering through images of the framework's personality.

The Heartbeat of London

Today, the London Underground contains 11 lines, 270 stations, and more than 250 miles of track, making it one of the biggest and most mind boggling metropolitan travel frameworks on the planet. It fills in as an imperative course for London's regular routine, working with the development of roughly 5,000,000 travellers every day.

The Cylinder's job reaches out past simple transportation. It is a social balancer, utilised by individuals from varying backgrounds, from workers and vacationers to understudies and experts. Its span interfaces the city's assorted areas, social milestones, and business centres, making it essential to London's social and monetary texture.

Exploring the Organization

Exploring the London Underground can at first appear to be overwhelming because of its intricacy, however the framework is planned considering ease of use. The famous Cylinder map improves on route, utilising a variety of coded lines and clear station names to direct travellers. Significant trade stations, like Lord's Cross St Pancras, Oxford Bazaar, and Liverpool Road, work with consistent exchanges between lines, guaranteeing effective travel across the city.

The presentation of contactless instalment choices, for example, Shellfish cards and contactless bank cards, has smoothed out the admission framework, making it simple for travellers to jump on and off trains without the requirement for paper tickets. The Cylinder works with wonderful recurrence, with trains running like clockwork during busy times and an extensive Night Cylinder administration at the end of the week, guaranteeing the network even in the late hours.

Compositional and Social Tourist spots

The London Underground isn't simply a method of transport; it is a grandstand of engineering and social legacy. Many stations, like the craftsmanship deco works of art at Arnos Woods and Southgate, and the innovator plan of Canary Wharf, are commended for their tasteful allure. The multifaceted tiling and mosaics at stations like Cook Road and Tottenham Court Street mirror the city's imaginative style.

Public craftsmanship establishments, for example, the "Workmanship on the Underground" program, carry contemporary workmanship to suburbanites, changing ordinary excursions into socially advancing encounters. Remarkable works incorporate the energetic paintings at Brixton station and the striking mosaics at Tottenham Court Street.

Difficulties and Developments

In spite of its numerous assets, the London Underground faces continuous difficulties, including maturing framework, limit requirements, and the requirement for consistent support. The city's populace development and expanding ridership request constant speculation and advancement to guarantee the framework stays proficient and dependable.

Ongoing drives, for example, the development of the Elizabeth Line (Crossrail), intend to mitigate blockage and further develop availability by adding new courses and extending the organization. Moves up to flagging frameworks and the presentation of cooled trains on a few lines improve traveller solace and functional productivity.

The Tube likewise assumes a significant part in London's manageability endeavours. By giving a productive option in contrast to vehicle travel, it diminishes gridlock and lowers ozone-harming substance emanations, adding to the city's natural objectives.

Buses

London's transports are something other than a method for getting from point A to point B; they are a fundamental area of the city's character, winding through its roads with a set of experiences as rich and vivid as the actual city. Conspicuous around the world, these red two layers are an image of London's mix of custom and development. This exposition investigates the set of experiences, importance, and current effect of London's transport framework.

A Verifiable Viewpoint

The account of London's transports starts in the mid nineteenth hundred years. The primary pony drawn omnibus assistance began in 1829, worked by George Shillibeer. These early transports could convey up to 22 travellers and were a prompt achievement, giving another degree of versatility for Londoners. As the city extended, so did the transport organisation, turning into a fundamental piece of day to day existence.

The genuine change came in the mid twentieth 100 years with the presentation of mechanised transports. The notable red multi level buses made their presentation during the 1920s, changing public vehicle. The AEC Routemaster, presented in 1956, turned into the most popular model, with its unmistakable plan and open back stage permitting travellers to jump on and off easily.

The Image of London

The Routemaster immediately turned into an image of London, catching the creative mind of local people and vacationers the same. Its plan was both utilitarian and stylish, with a design that boosted seating limit while keeping up with mobility on London's thin roads. The transports were painted in a striking red, a variety that has since become inseparable from London's transport armada.

Throughout the long term, the picture of the red multi level bus has been deified in movies, postcards, and keepsakes, addressing the soul of

London. Indeed, even as present day models supplanted the Routemaster, its inheritance perseveres, with a couple of as yet working on legacy courses for those nostalgic for the past.

Current Developments

Today, London's transport framework is perhaps of the most progressive and broad on the planet. The organisation contains more than 700 courses, serving a great many travellers day to day. Present day transports are planned in view of availability, highlighting low floors for simple boarding, need seating, and space for wheelchairs and buggies.

Innovation has likewise changed the transport insight. Constant following permits travellers to see live updates on transport appearance times by means of applications and computerized shows at transport stops. Contactless instalment frameworks, including Shellfish cards and contactless bank cards, have smoothed out admission assortment, making transport travel more productive and easy to understand.

Ecological supportability is a critical concentration for London's transport organization. The city has acquainted mixture and electric transports with decrease emanations and further develop air quality. The obligation to green vehicle lines up with London's more extensive endeavors to battle environmental change and advance practical metropolitan living.

Social Effect

Transports are something beyond transportation; they are a social peculiarity. They give a novel vantage highlight investigating London's milestones, from the Pinnacle of London to Buckingham Royal residence. Vacationers frequently select multi level bus visits to encounter the city's sights according to a raised viewpoint.

Transports likewise assume an essential part in the day to day routines of Londoners, associating neighborhoods and networks. They give a reasonable and solid method of transport, fundamental for driving to work, school, or social exercises. The transport network is a help for the majority, especially in regions not served by the Underground.

The plan and activity of London's transports mirror the city's variety and inclusivity. Multilingual signage and sound declarations take care of the city's global populace, while night transports guarantee that London stays open nonstop.

Challenges and What's in store

Regardless of its triumphs, London's transport framework faces difficulties. Gridlock stays a critical issue, influencing transport dependability and unwavering quality. The city is tending to this with measures, for example, committed transport paths and blockage charges to focus on open vehicle.

The Coronavirus pandemic likewise presented exceptional difficulties, with diminished ridership and the requirement for improved wellbeing measures. Nonetheless, London's strength and flexibility have seen the transport network keep on serving its populace, showing its basic job in metropolitan portability.

Planning ahead, London expects to additional upgrade its transport organisation. Plans incorporate growing electric and hydrogen transport armadas, further developing openness, and coordinating innovation to give a consistent travel insight. These endeavors guarantee that London's transport will keep on developing, addressing the requirements of a developing and dynamic city.

Trams

Cable cars, frequently seen coasting along city roads and through tourist detours, are something beyond a method of transportation; they are an image of metropolitan appeal, verifiable heritage, and current proficiency. From their origin in the nineteenth 100 years to their resurgence in contemporary urban communities, cable cars play had an essential impact in molding public travel frameworks around the world. This paper digs into the set of experiences, benefits, and fate of cable cars, featuring their persevering through allure and importance.

A Verifiable Excursion

The historical backdrop of cable cars traces all the way back to the mid nineteenth century when horse-drawn cable cars made their presentation in urban communities like New York and London.

These early renditions gave a smoother and more agreeable ride contrasted with the unpleasant cobblestone roads. The presentation of electric cable cars in the late nineteenth-century upset metropolitan vehicles. Urban communities like Berlin, Budapest, and San Francisco immediately embraced this advancement, which took into consideration quicker and more proficient travel.

Electric cable cars turned into a staple of public travel in numerous urban communities all over the planet. They worked with driving as well as prodded metropolitan improvement by interfacing already out of reach regions. Notorious cable car frameworks, similar to those in Melbourne, Vienna, and Lisbon, became basic to the cityscapes, mixing usefulness with stylish allure.

Benefits of Cable cars

Cable cars offer various benefits that make them a favored method of transport in current urban communities. One of the main advantages is their ecological benevolence. Cable cars are regularly controlled by power, which lessens ozone depleting substance emanations and reliance on petroleum derivatives. This makes them a practical choice, particularly with regards to developing worries about environmental change and metropolitan contamination.

One more key benefit is their ability to lighten gridlock. Cable cars can convey countless travelers, decreasing the quantity of vehicles out and about and facilitating traffic stream. This is especially significant in thickly populated metropolitan regions where street space is restricted. Moreover, cable cars work on devoted tracks, keeping away from the postpones that transports and vehicles frequently face because of gridlocks.

Cable cars additionally improve metropolitan availability. They can explore through thin roads and sharp corners, giving admittance to regions that different types of public vehicle probably won't reach. This makes them ideal for noteworthy downtown areas and thickly constructed areas.

Additionally, cable car stops are generally nearer together than metro or train stations, offering more helpful access for travelers.

Cable cars in the Advanced Time

The resurgence of cable cars in the 21st century mirrors a recharged interest in supportable and proficient public vehicle. Urban communities all over the planet are putting resources into cable car organisations to address the difficulties of metropolitan versatility. Current cable cars are outfitted with trend setting innovation, including constant following, low-floor plans for openness, and energy-productive frameworks.

In Europe, urban communities like Amsterdam, Berlin, and Prague have broad cable car networks that are basic to their public vehicle frameworks. In North America, urban communities, for example, Toronto and San Francisco keep up with notorious cable car benefits that draw in the two workers and vacationers. Indeed, even in Asia, urban areas like Hong Kong and Melbourne have embraced cable cars as a component of their metropolitan scene, offering tourist detours and dependable help.

The allure of cable cars stretches out past their common sense. They are many times seen as an image of a city's personality and history. The one of a kind cable cars of Lisbon, with their particular yellow tone and beguiling clatter, bring out sentimentality and draw in vacationers. The smooth, current cable cars of Zurich and Helsinki address the front line of metropolitan travel innovation.

The Eventual fate of Cable cars

The eventual fate of cable cars looks encouraging as urban communities keep on looking for supportable and proficient vehicle arrangements. Advancements, for example, battery-controlled cable cars and remote charging innovation are being created to additionally decrease natural effect and functional expenses. Additionally, the incorporation of cable cars with different methods of transport, like transports, bikes, and walker pathways, is making more strong and easy to use travel frameworks.

Cable cars likewise assume a vital part in the vision of shrewd urban communities. With the approach of advanced innovation, cable cars are turning out to be important for an interconnected metropolitan environment. Savvy tagging, constant traveller data, and information driven help improvement are upgrading the general travel insight. These headways further develop effectiveness as well as add to the more extensive objectives of metropolitan maintainability and decency.

River Services

London, a city prestigious for its famous milestones and rich history, offers a remarkable method for investigating its heart through its broad stream administrations. The Thames, twisting through the city, isn't simply a pleasant stream however a crucial corridor for transportation and the travel industry. This article dives into the advantages and encounters of utilizing London's waterway administrations, featuring why they are a fundamental area of the city's dynamic foundation.

A Verifiable Point of View

The Thames has been vital to London's improvement for a really long time, filling in as a significant course for exchange, safeguard, and correspondence. From the Roman period to the current day, the stream has seen the advancement of the city. Today, while it no longer fills in as the essential method for transport for merchandise, it stays a pivotal part of London's public vehicle organization and a famous fascination for vacationers.

The Advanced Stream Administration Organization

London's waterway administrations are worked by different suppliers, with Transport for London (TfL) supervising a significant part of the organization.

The essential administrations incorporate suburbanite boats, recreation travels, and confidential sanctions, each taking care of various necessities.

Worker Administrations: The Thames Trimmers, a piece of the TfL organisation, give normal suburbanite administrations between central issues along the stream. These high velocity sailboats offer a solid and grand option in contrFor workers, these administrations offer a peaceful excursion, liberated from the clog and postpones frequently experienced on the streets and underground.

Relaxation Travels: For vacationers and local people the same, recreation travels offer a loosening up method for encountering London's milestones from the water. Organisations like City Travels and Bateaux London give a scope of touring visits, feasting travels, and themed occasions. These travels frequently incorporate discourse, giving travellers experiences into the set of experiences and meaning of the tourist spots they pass, like the Pinnacle of London, the Places of Parliament, and the notable Pinnacle Extension.

Confidential Sanctions: For extraordinary events or custom encounters, confidential contracts are accessible. These administrations take into consideration modified courses and schedules, making them ideal for corporate occasions, weddings, or individual festivals. Extravagance boats and yachts can be employed, giving a selective method for partaking in the Thames and its environmental elements.

Key Advantages of Waterway Administrations

Beautiful Perspectives: One of the most convincing motivations to utilise waterway administrations is the unrivalled perspectives they offer. Going by boat gives an interesting viewpoint of the city's horizon and milestones, a considerable lot of which are best valued from the water. Whether it's the cutting edge engineering of the Shard or the memorable loftiness of the Royal residence of Westminster, the visual experience is unrivaled.

Accommodation and Availability: The stream administrations are very much incorporated with London's more extensive vehicle organisation. Key wharfs are situated close to significant attractions and transport centers, making it simple to switch among stream and land transport. For example, Bank Wharf is near Charing Cross Station, while North Greenwich Dock serves the O2 Field.

Unwinding and Solace: Contrasted with the frequently jam-packed transports and trains, stream administrations give a more loose and roomy climate. Travellers can appreciate outside decks or agreeable indoor seating, frequently with installed rewards accessible. This makes waterway travel not simply a method for getting from point A to point B, yet a lovely involvement with itself.

Ecological Advantages: Waterway administrations are likewise a greener option in contrast to street transport, assisting with lessening gridlock and lower discharges. Numerous cutting edge vessels are planned with eco-accommodating innovations, adding to a more practical metropolitan vehicle framework.

Novel Encounters

London's waterway administrations offer something beyond transport; they give extraordinary encounters that take special care of different interests:

Verifiable Visits: Specific travels, like those zeroing in on London's sea history, offer profound jumps into the city's past. These visits frequently incorporate stops at verifiable locales like the Cutty Sark in Greenwich or the Exhibition hall of London Docklands.

Feasting and Diversion: Supper travels join connoisseurs eating with live diversion, offering a noteworthy method for celebrating exceptional events. As you coast along the Thames, you can appreciate fine food and live exhibitions, all while taking in the enlightened horizon.

Occasional Occasions: Consistently, the stream has various occasions and themed travels. From light shows on New Year's Eve to happy Christmas travels, there's continuously something exceptional occurring on the Thames.

Taxis and Ride-Sharing

In the clamouring universe of metropolitan transportation, taxicabs and ride-sharing administrations assume vital parts in forming how individuals travel through urban areas. These methods of transport offer comfort, adaptability, and openness, taking special care of assorted needs and inclinations. This article investigates the advancement, advantages, and difficulties of cabs and ride-sharing administrations, featuring their effect on current metropolitan portability.

The Development of Cabs

Taxis have been an indispensable piece of metropolitan transportation for more than a long period. The famous yellow taxis of New York City and the dark taxis of London are not simply vehicles; they are social images. The idea of employing a confidential vehicle traces all the way back to the mid seventeenth 100 years with horse-drawn carriages, developing into mechanized taxis in the late nineteenth and mid twentieth hundreds of years.

Customary cabs are directed by nearby state run administrations, guaranteeing normalised admissions, driver capabilities, and vehicle wellbeing. This guideline gives a degree of unwavering quality and trust for travellers. Besides, cabbies frequently have broad information on city roads, making them adroit at exploring through traffic and finding the speediest courses.

The Ascent of Ride-Sharing Administrations

The approach of ride-sharing administrations, spearheaded by organizations like Uber and Lyft, changed metropolitan transportation. Sent off in the mid 2010s, these stages influence cell phone innovation and GPS to associate travelers with neighbouring drivers. This development has changed the manner in which individuals hail rides, offering a consistent and easy to use insight.

Ride-sharing administrations give a few benefits over conventional taxicabs. They offer ongoing following, credit only installments, and straightforward estimating. Travelers can rate drivers, making a criticism circle that energizes high help norms. Moreover, ride-sharing applications frequently have highlights like carpooling, which diminish costs and natural effects by imparting rides to others heading in a similar bearing.

Advantages of Cabs and Ride-Sharing

The two taxicabs and ride-sharing administrations carry various advantages to metropolitan transportation.

1. Convenience and Openness: With the tap of a button, travellers can bring a ride to their precise area, making travel more available, particularly in regions with restricted public transportation choices.

2. Flexibility: Not at all like fixed-course open travel, cabs and ride-sharing administrations offer house to house administration, giving a more significant level of adaptability and comfort.

3. Economic Open doors: Ride-sharing has set out work open doors for some people, permitting drivers to work adaptable hours and acquire pay through gig economy stages.

4. Safety and Security: The two cabs and ride-sharing administrations have carried out wellbeing measures, for example, GPS following, driver historical verifications, and crisis help highlights, improving traveller security.

Difficulties and Debates

Regardless of their benefits, taxicabs and ride-sharing administrations face a few difficulties and contentions.

1. Regulation and Fair Rivalry: The ascent of ride-sharing has started banters about the guideline and fair contest. Conventional taxi administrators contend that ride-sharing organizations frequently work with less administrative weights, prompting a lopsided battleground. States are consistently attempting to find an equilibrium that guarantees security and decency for all gatherings included.

2. Safety Worries: While the two taxicabs and ride-sharing administrations have wellbeing conventions, episodes of wrongdoing and mishaps can happen. Guaranteeing thorough historical verifications, driver preparing, and traveler security highlights stay critical.

3. Impact on Traffic and Climate: The comfort of ride-sharing can add to expanded gridlock and contamination, especially in thickly

populated metropolitan regions. Nonetheless, carpooling and electric vehicle choices are relieving factors that a few stages are advancing.

4. Driver Government assistance: The gig economy nature of ride-sharing frequently implies drivers need advantages like health care coverage, paid leave, and employer stability. Tending to these worries is crucial for economical business rehearses inside the business.

The Eventual fate of Metropolitan Transportation

The fate of taxicabs and ride-sharing administrations will probably see further incorporation of innovation and maintainability drives. Independent vehicles (AVs) are ready to change the two ventures, promising more secure, more productive rides. Ride-sharing organizations are now putting resources into AV innovation, planning to lessen costs and further develop administration dependability.

Manageability will likewise assume a critical part, with a push towards electric vehicles (EVs) to decrease carbon impressions. State-run administrations and organizations are progressively teaming up to foster a foundation that upholds EVs, making harmless ecosystem transportation more reasonable.

Cycling

Cycling in London has developed emphatically over the course of the last ten years, changing the city into an energetic and cyclist-accommodating city. From committed bicycle paths to panoramic detours and creative bicycle sharing projects, London offers a special viewpoint for those ready to investigate it on two wheels. This exposition dives into the justifications for why cycling in London is an energizing, effective, and agreeable method for encountering the city.

The Ascent of Cycling Foundation

London has put altogether in cycling framework, making it more secure and more helpful for cyclists. The presentation of Cycle Interstates — committed, nonstop bicycle paths interfacing key region of the city — has been a unique advantage. Courses like CS3, running from Yelping to Lancaster Entryway, and CS6, interfacing Elephant and Palace to Ruler's Cross, furnish cyclists with protected, direct ways that keep away from weighty traffic.

Notwithstanding these expressways, the city has executed Quietways, which are less bustling courses that utilization calmer roads and green spaces. These courses are ideally suited for the individuals who lean toward an all the more comfortable ride away from the hurrying around of the fundamental streets.

Bicycle Sharing Projects

One of the most open ways of going in London is through its bicycle sharing projects. The Santander Cycles, normally known as "Boris Bicycles" after the previous city chairman Boris Johnson who presented them, offer a helpful and reasonable method for getting around. With docking stations spread all through the city, you can undoubtedly get and drop off a bicycle any place you are.

For the individuals who favor electric help, the as of late presented e-bicycle programs give an additional lift, making it simpler to handle London's intermittent slopes and longer distances gracefully.

Investigating London's Milestones by Bicycle

Cycling offers an interesting and vivid method for encountering London's famous tourist spots. A ride along the Thames Way gives dazzling perspectives on the waterway and passes by key attractions like the Pinnacle of London, Tate Present day, and the London Eye. Going through Hyde Park and Kensington Nurseries offers a picturesque and serene departure, with courses taking you past the Serpentine Lake and the Diana, Princess of Ribs Dedication Wellspring.

For a mix of history and culture, a ride through the City of London and Westminster is great. You can cycle past St. Paul's Church building, the Places of Parliament, and Buckingham Castle, appreciating the city's rich engineering legacy from a one of a kind vantage point.

Green Spaces and Tourist detours

London's broad organisation of parks and green spaces makes cycling a joy. Official's Park, with its expansive roads and beautiful nurseries, is ideal for a loosening up ride. Richmond Park, quite possibly of the biggest green space in the city, offers a more tough involvement in its crowds of deer and far reaching sees over London.

The Wandle Trail, following the Stream Wandle from Croydon to the Thames, joins metropolitan and provincial scenes, making it a number one for nature sweethearts. The Lee Valley Local Park, extending from East London to Hertfordshire, offers north of 26 miles of spinning ways through wetlands, parklands, and repositories.

Wellbeing and Ecological Advantages

Cycling in London isn't just charming yet in addition useful for wellbeing and the climate. Normal cycling works on cardiovascular wellness, fortifies muscles, and improves mental prosperity. It is a low-influence practice reasonable for individuals, all things considered, making it a comprehensive action.

Earth cycling decreases fossil fuel byproducts and gridlock, adding to cleaner air and a greener city. By deciding to cycle, Londoners and guests can have an impact in making a more reasonable and eco-accommodating metropolitan climate.

Difficulties and Contemplations

While cycling in London enjoys many benefits, it is critical to know about the difficulties. The city's bustling roads can be scary for unpracticed cyclists, and the weather conditions can be eccentric. Notwithstanding, with appropriate preparation and precautionary measures, these difficulties can be made due. Wearing a head protector, utilising lights and intelligent stuff, and getting to know cycling courses and traffic rules are fundamental for a protected ride.

Walking Tours

London, with its rich history, energetic culture, and different areas, is a city best investigated by walking. Strolling visits offer a one of a kind and vivid method for encountering the city's appeal, giving bits of knowledge and stories that you could miss in any case. This exposition digs into the appeal of strolling visits in London, featuring the various sorts of visits accessible, the advantages of investigating by walking, and some priority courses for each explorer.

The Advantages of Strolling Visits

Strolling visits offer a few benefits over different types of touring. First and foremost, they permit you to encounter the city at a comfortable speed, allowing you the opportunity to ingest your environmental elements really. Strolling through London's roads, you can interruption to respect building subtleties, jump into curious shops, and chat with local people.

Strolling visits are additionally harmless to the ecosystem, diminishing the carbon impression related with different methods of transportation. Furthermore, they frequently give more private and connecting with encounters, drove by learned guides who can share entrancing stories, verifiable realities, and unlikely treasures that are excluded from manuals.

Verifiable Strolling Visits

London's rich history is best valued through its roads and milestones. Verifiable strolling visits take guests on an excursion through time, investigating huge locales and telling stories of the past.

• The City of London Visit: This visit covers the most established piece of London, where you can visit the Pinnacle of London, St. Paul's Church building, and the leftovers of the Roman Wall. Guides share accounts of middle age London, the Incomparable Fire of 1666, and the city's development into a worldwide monetary center.

• The Westminster Visit: This visit incorporates famous milestones like Buckingham Castle, the Places of Parliament, and Westminster Nunnery. It offers bits of knowledge into English governmental issues, illustrious history, and the engineering quality of these prestigious designs.

Artistic and Social Visits

For writing and culture fans, strolling visits zeroed in on London's imaginative legacy give a more profound enthusiasm for the city's commitments to human expression.

• The Shakespeare and Dickens Visit: This visit investigates regions related with William Shakespeare and Charles Dickens. Visit the Globe Theater, where Shakespeare's plays were performed, and stroll through Dickensian London, visiting destinations that motivated his books, for example, the Old Interest Shop and Saffron Slope.

• The Harry Potter Visit: An enchanted excursion for fanatics of J.K. Rowling's wizarding world, this visit incorporates areas utilized in the Harry Potter films, for example, Stage 9¾ at Ruler's Cross Station and the Leadenhall Market, which filled in as Diagon Back street.

Themed Strolling Visits

Themed strolling visits take care of specialty interests, offering novel viewpoints on the city.

• The Jack the Ripper Visit: Dig into the dull history of Victorian London with a visit that follows the means of the notorious Jack the Ripper. Guides describe the grim subtleties of the homicides and the secret encompassing the unidentified executioner.

• The Road Craftsmanship Visit: London is a material for a portion of the world's best road specialists. This visit takes you through dynamic areas like Shoreditch and Camden, exhibiting staggering paintings and spray painting craftsmanship, and examining the specialists behind them, including the tricky Banksy.

Neighbourhood Strolling Visits

Investigating explicit areas by walking permits you to encounter their unmistakable characters and nearby life.

• The Notting Slope Visit: Well known for its vivid houses, enchanting shops, and the clamoring Portobello Street Market, Notting Slope offers a pleasant and enthusiastic walk. Find the historical backdrop of the region and its change into perhaps of London's trendiest area.

• The Greenwich Visit: A stroll through Greenwich incorporates the Cutty Sark, the

Imperial Observatory, and the shocking Greenwich Park. This visit joins oceanic history with amazing perspectives on the London horizon.

Independent Strolling Visits

For the people who like to investigate at their own speed, independent strolling visits offer adaptability and the opportunity to wait in spots of revenue. Various applications and manuals give itemized courses and data, permitting you to autonomously explore the city.

Accessibility Tips

London, a city known for its rich history, different culture, and energetic energy, endeavors to be a comprehensive objective for all explorers. Whether you have versatility challenges, visual or hearing hindrances, or other openness needs, London offers a scope of administrations and offices to guarantee your visit is charming and bother free.

This paper gives complete tips to exploring London effortlessly and solace.

Exploring Public Vehicle

London's public vehicle framework is broad and ceaselessly working on its availability. The Vehicle for London (TfL) site and the TfL Go application are important assets, giving itemised data on open courses and administrations.

1. Transports:
London's transports are all wheelchair open, including slopes and assigned spaces for wheelchair clients. General media declarations are standard, supporting those with visual or hearing hindrances. Transport stops are intended to be open, with material clearing and clear signage.

2. Underground:
While not all Cylinder stations are completely available, the organization is getting to the next level. At present, around 33% of the 270 stations have sans step access from road to stage. TfL

gives a Cylinder map featuring open stations, and manual boarding inclines are accessible at numerous areas.

3. Overground and DLR:
The London Overground and Docklands Light Railroad (DLR) are more open than the Cylinder. Most stations have sans step access, and the trains are planned with low floors to work with boarding.

4. Taxicabs and Ride-Sharing:
London's famous dark taxis are wheelchair open and can be hailed in the city or booked through telephone. Moreover, ride-sharing administrations like Uber offer choices for travelers with openness needs.

Convenience

Numerous lodgings in London take special care of visitors with handicaps, offering highlights, for example, sans step doors, open washrooms, and adjusted rooms. While booking, search for inns that show their availability qualifications plainly. Sites like Booking.com and Expedia permit you to channel query items by availability highlights.

Attractions

1. Historical centers and Displays:
London's historical centers and displays, including the English Exhibition hall, the Public Exhibition, and the Tate Present day, are focused on availability. Most have sans step access, open latrines, and offices for guests with tangible weaknesses, for example, material shows and sound aides. A few organizations, similar to the Victoria and Albert Gallery, offer gesture based communication visits and contact visits.

2. Theaters and Films:
West End theaters and films across London are turning out to be progressively open. Settings frequently give wheelchair spaces, hearing circles, and inscribed or sound depicted exhibitions. It's prudent to contact the setting ahead of time to guarantee your requirements are met.

3. Stops and Open Spaces:

London's parks, including Hyde Park, Official's Park, and the Regal Botanic Nurseries at Kew, offer available pathways, debilitated stopping, and offices, for example, open latrines and portability bike employ. Kew Nurseries, for instance, gives a bus administration to assist guests with versatility issues explore the broad grounds.

Shopping and Feasting

1. Shopping:

Significant shopping regions like Oxford Road, Official Road, and Westfield Retail outlet are furnished with sans step access, lifts, and available latrines. Stores and malls frequently offer extra types of assistance like individual shopping associates for guests with handicaps.

2. Eating:

Numerous cafés and bistros in London are available, with sans step doorways and adjusted offices. Sites like OpenTable and Cry permit you to look for available eating choices. For explicit dietary necessities, the city offers a different scope of eateries taking special care of sans gluten, veggie lover, and other dietary prerequisites.

Extra Tips

1. Preparing:
Prior to your outing, explore and plan your schedule considering availability. Sites like AccessAble give definite access to advisers for a huge number of settings across London. The Visit London site additionally offers openness data for vacationers.

2. Help Administrations:
On the off chance that you need support, administrations like Traveler Help (for train travel) and TfL's Movement Tutoring Administration can give assistance. It's likewise helpful to convey a RADAR key, which gives admittance to locked open latrines across the city.

3. Crisis Contacts:

If there should be an occurrence of crises, guarantee you have a rundown of contacts for neighbourhood medical care su

Chapter 4: Where to Stay

Picking where to stay in London can be overpowering given the city's tremendous size and various areas. Whether you're searching for extravagance, history, culture, or neighborhood beguile, London offers facilities to suit each inclination and financial plan. This exposition gives a point by point manual for probably the best regions to remain in London, guaranteeing a paramount visit to the English capital.

1. Covent Garden: The Core of Theater and Amusement

Covent Garden is perhaps London's most lively area, known for its clamouring piazza, road entertainers, and a variety of shops, eateries, and bars. Remaining here places you in the core of London's West End, home to widely popular

135

theaters and shows. The Regal Drama House and incalculably different settings make it a social center.

• Aces: Focal area, vivacious air, near significant attractions like the English Exhibition hall and Trafalgar Square.
• Cons: Can be uproarious and swarmed, particularly in the nights.

2. Soho: Nightlife and Eating Area of interest

For the people who blossom with nightlife and culinary enjoyments, Soho is the spot to be. This varied area offers a blend of popular bars, notable bars, and various cafés, from very good quality eating to particular bistros. It's likewise a short distance from Oxford Road, London's chief shopping objective.

• Professionals: Energising nightlife, different feasting choices, near significant shopping regions.

- Cons: Occupied and uproarious, particularly on ends of the week.

3. South Bank: Riverside Culture and Perspectives

South Bank is great for culture aficionados, with milestones like the Tate Present day, Shakespeare's Globe, and the Southbank Center. The region offers shocking perspectives on the Thames and notorious designs like the London Eye. It's an extraordinary spot for relaxed riverside strolls and absorbing the imaginative environment.

- Experts: Social attractions, delightful stream sees, less touristy feel.
- Cons: Can be calmer around evening time, somewhat further from a few focal attractions.

4. Kensington and Chelsea: Extravagance and Style

For a sample of extravagance and refinement, Kensington and Chelsea are the neighborhoods to consider. Home to upscale stores, top notch exhibition halls like the Victoria and Albert Gallery and the Regular History Historical center, and rich garden squares, this region radiates refinement.

• Experts: Upscale facilities, near significant galleries, lovely private roads.
• Cons: Costly, less lively nightlife.

5. Bloomsbury: Scholarly and Artistic Appeal

Bloomsbury, known for its scholarly history and scholastic establishments, offers a calmer yet halfway found choice. Home to the English Historical center and various bookshops, this area has an insightful climate. It's likewise near the College of London and the English Library.

• Stars: Focal yet calmer, wealthy in abstract history, near exhibition halls.
• Cons: Less nightlife choices, more private.

6. Shoreditch: Stylish and Imaginative

Shoreditch is the focal point of London's innovative and tech scenes. Known for its energetic road workmanship, free stores, and hip bistros, it draws in a more youthful, imaginative group. The region is likewise popular for its nightlife, with a wealth of bars, clubs, and unrecorded music scenes.

• Professionals: Popular and imaginative energy, vivacious nightlife, incredible food scene.
• Cons: Can be clearly and swarmed, particularly at the end of the week.

7. Westminster: Notorious Milestones and History

Remaining in Westminster places you in closeness to a portion of London's most notable milestones, including Buckingham Castle, the Places of Parliament, and Westminster Nunnery. This region is great for first-time guests who need to be close to the city's significant attractions and noteworthy destinations.

• Experts: Near significant tourist spots, wealthy ever, focal area.
• Cons: Exceptionally touristy, can be costly.

8. Camden: Option and Bohemian

Camden is famous for its elective culture, clamoring markets, and lively music scene. The Camden Market offers a diverse blend of rare style, specialties, and global food slows down. It's an extraordinary region for those looking for a bohemian environment and a break from the standard.

• Experts: Novel and elective culture, incredible business sectors, enthusiastic music scene.

- Cons: Can be packed, particularly at the end of the week.

Neighbourhoods and Districts

London, a rambling city, is a mosaic of particular areas and regions, each with its own special appeal and character. From noteworthy regions reverberating with exceptionally old stories to dynamic, present day locale beating with contemporary energy, London offers a rich and differed metropolitan embroidery. This paper digs into probably the most enthralling areas and locale, showing why they are fundamental stops on any visit to the city.

Westminster: The Core of History and Power

Westminster is the focal point of English political life and a gold mine of verifiable tourist spots. Here, guests can wonder about the notorious Places of Parliament and Large Ben, structures that represent English majority rule government. Westminster Monastery, the site of regal crowning ceremonies and weddings, offers a brief look into the country's celebrated past. The region likewise incorporates Buckingham Castle, the authority home of the ruler, where the Top-down restructuring function is a priority occasion.

St. James' Park, one of London's imperial parks, gives a tranquil green space in the midst of the magnificence, ideal for a relaxed walk. The region's authentic importance and structural wonder make Westminster a fundamental stop for any guest trying to grasp London's legacy.

Covent Nursery: A Center point of Culture and Diversion

Covent Nursery, when a clamouring products of the soil market, has changed into a dynamic social and diversion region. The region is renowned for its road entertainers, who engage swarms with music, enchantment, and tumbling. The noteworthy market fabricating now houses store shops, craftsman slows down, and an assortment of eating choices, making it an ideal spot for a comfortable outing.

The Regal Drama House, an incredibly famous scene, offers heavenly exhibitions of show and expressive dance. The close by Theater Regal Drury Path, perhaps of the most established venue on the planet, keeps on facilitating acclaimed creations. Covent Nursery's exuberant environment, joined with its rich social contributions, makes it a #1 among local people and travellers the same.

Soho: The Beat of Nightlife and Inventiveness

Soho, situated in the West End, is the thumping heart of London's nightlife and imaginative scene. This varied area is loaded with popular bars, clubs, and music scenes, offering diversion sometime later. Famous settings like Ronnie Scott's Jazz Club and the Soho Theater grandstand a scope of exhibitions, from unrecorded music to state of the art satire.

Soho is likewise a culinary area of interest, with a variety of eateries serving foods from around the world. From conventional English bars to stylish global restaurants, the feasting choices are pretty much as different as the actual locals. The region's energetic energy and imaginative pizazz make Soho a must-visit for those looking for a sample of London's contemporary culture.

Shoreditch: The Apex of Trendy person Cool

Shoreditch, in East London, has gone through a sensational change from a modern region to an in vogue, creative territory. Known for its energetic road craftsmanship, including works by the slippery Banksy, Shoreditch is a safe house for creatives and pioneers. The region is loaded up with autonomous stores, one of a kind shops, and state of the art exhibitions, mirroring its vanguard soul.

Block Path, a popular road in Shoreditch, is prestigious for its curry houses and idiosyncratic business sectors. The Old Truman Bottling works has different occasions, from style markets to craftsmanship presentations, adding to the local's powerful air. Shoreditch's mix of restless inventiveness and verifiable roots makes it a convincing objective for guests.

Notting Slope: An Enchanting and Vivid Getaway

Notting Slope, made well known by the eponymous film, is quite possibly London's most pleasant area. Its pastel-shaded houses and curious roads make a beguiling, town-like air. Portobello Street Market, one of the world's biggest collectibles markets, draws swarms looking for extraordinary fortunes and rare finds.

The yearly Notting Slope Festival, an energetic festival of Caribbean culture, changes the roads into an uproar of variety, music, and dance. The local's blend of appeal, culture, and local area soul makes Notting Slope a great region to investigate.

South Bank: A Riverside Social Quarter

South Bank, extending along the Waterway Thames, is a social area of interest offering staggering perspectives and a plenty of attractions. The Southbank Center, which incorporates the Illustrious Celebration Corridor, the Hayward Display, and the Public Theater, has a different scope of exhibitions and presentations. The region is additionally home to the famous London Eye, giving all encompassing perspectives on the city.

The riverside walkways are fixed with road entertainers, food slows down, and spring up business sectors, making an energetic climate. The close by Tate Current, housed in a changed over power station, features contemporary craftsmanship from around the world. South Bank's mix of social establishments and grand excellence makes it a must-visit locale.

Camden: A Mixture of Elective Culture

Camden, in North London, is inseparable from elective culture and varied markets. Camden Market, a rambling complex of slows down and shops, offers everything from one of a kind dress and high quality specialties to worldwide road food. The local's underground rock legacy is as yet clear in its tense design and dynamic music scene.

Camden Lock, a pleasant trench region, gives a peaceful departure from the clamoring roads. The Electric Dance hall and the Roundhouse are famous music settings that have facilitated amazing exhibitions. Camden's one of a kind mix of nonconformity and innovativeness makes it an interesting region to investigate.

Central London

Central London, a clamouring region that typifies the embodiment of one of the world's most powerful urban communities, is a must-visit for any voyager. Home to notable landmarks, social fortunes, and dynamic areas, Central London offers an unmatched encounter that consolidates history, craftsmanship, trade, and amusement. This paper investigates the numerous features that make Central London an outstanding objective.

Historical Landmarks

Central London is saturated with history, with landmarks that have endured over the extreme long haul. The Places of Parliament and Enormous Ben are maybe the most conspicuous images of English majority rules system and administration. The grand Westminster Nunnery, an UNESCO World Legacy Site, has been the crowning ordinance church for English rulers beginning around 1066 and is the last resting place for the vast majority eminent figures.

The Pinnacle of London, another UNESCO site, offers a brief look into the city's middle age past. This stronghold plays served different parts, from regal home to jail, and is home to the Royal gems. Close by, the notable Pinnacle Scaffold traverses the Thames, its Victorian Gothic design a striking differentiation to the cutting edge horizon.

Social and Creative Center points

Central London is a social force to be reckoned with, flaunting top notch exhibition halls, displays, and theatres. The English Gallery, with its immense assortment of workmanship and relics, takes guests on an excursion through mankind's set of experiences. The Public Exhibition, situated in Trafalgar Square, houses show-stoppers by specialists like Van Gogh, Rembrandt, and Leonardo da Vinci.

For contemporary craftsmanship fans, the Tate Current, housed in a previous power station, offers state of the art displays and establishments. Theatre sweethearts will track down no lack of diversion in the West End, where long-running musicals, exemplary plays, and new creations elegance the phases of memorable scenes like the Imperial Drama House and the Globe Theater, a loyal remaking of Shakespeare's playhouse.

Shopping and Feasting

Central London is a customer's heaven, offering everything from extravagance shops to mixed markets. Oxford Road, Official Road, and Bond Road are popular for their very good quality stores and lead shops. For a more remarkable shopping experience, Covent Nursery consolidates road entertainers, creator shops, and distinctive business sectors in a beguiling setting.

The feasting scene in Central London mirrors its multicultural person. From Michelin-featured eateries like The Ledbury and Sketch to dynamic food markets like District Market, the region takes care of all preferences and spending plans. Customary English charge can be delighted in at memorable bars, while worldwide cooking styles have large amounts of areas like Soho and Chinatown.

Green Spaces and Beautiful Magnificence

In the midst of the metropolitan hustle, Central London offers desert springs of quietness in its parks and gardens. Hyde Park, perhaps the biggest green space in the city, furnishes a tranquil retreat with its Serpentine Lake, Speaker's Corner, and different landmarks. St. James' Park, nearby Buckingham Royal residence, offers staggering perspectives on the castle and the encompassing vegetation.

The South Bank of the Thames is one more beautiful spot, ideal for comfortable walks around perspectives on landmarks, for example, the London Eye, the Shard, and the Thousand YearsExtension. The riverbank is additionally home to social scenes like the Southbank Center and the Public Theater, adding to the area's lively climate.

Nightlife and Amusement

As the sun sets, Central London changes into a jungle gym of nightlife and diversion. The West End's auditoriums are only the start. Soho, known for its varied blend of bars, clubs, and eateries, offers an exuberant nightlife scene. Whether you incline toward a complex mixed drink bar, a conventional bar, or anin-vogue club, Central London has something for everybody.

Unrecorded music can be appreciated at notable scenes like the Illustrious Albert Lobby and the O2 Field, where incredibly famous specialists perform routinely. For a more cozy encounter, jazz clubs and independent music settings spot the region, exhibiting neighbourhood ability and worldwide demonstrations.

West End

The West End of London, frequently alluded to just as "The West End," is a lively region eminent for its theatres, social milestones, shopping objections, and nightlife. Similar to Broadway in New York City, the West End is a magnet for travelers and local people the same, offering a rich embroidery of diversion and culture. This article investigates the charm of the West End, its historical importance, its notorious theaters, and its part in contemporary culture.

A Historical Outline

The West End's set of experiences is profoundly interlaced with London's development as a worldwide social center point. The region started to foster in the seventeenth hundred years as a well-off locale, with terrific squares and exquisite homes. By the nineteenth hundred years, it had developed into a clamouring diversion region, loaded up with theatres, music corridors, and theatrical presentations. This change was pushed by the Modern Upset, which brought a deluge of individuals and abundance to the city.

The kickoff of theatres like the Theater Regal, Drury Path (worked in 1663), and the Illustrious Drama House (opened in 1732) set up for the West End's dramatic predominance. These settings facilitated everything from Shakespearean plays to dramas, establishing the region's standing as the focal point of London's social life.

The Venues of the West End

The West End brags a number of noteworthy cluster theatres, each with its novel appeal and historical importance. The Royal residence Theater, with its dazzling Victorian engineering, has been a foundation of the region starting around 1891. It right now has the well known "Harry Potter and the Reviled Youngster," drawing fans from around the world.

The Lyceum Theater, another notorious scene, has a rich history tracing all the way back to 1834. Today, it is inseparable from Disney's "The Lion Lord," a melodic that has enamoured crowds for more than twenty years with its dynamite outfits and extraordinary music.

The Apollo Victoria Theater is famous for its Craft Deco plan and long-running shows. It's the home of "Fiendish," a prequel to "The Wizard of Oz" that has become one of the most cherished musicals ever.

The West End isn't just about fantastic theatres. More modest scenes like the Donmar Distribution centre and the Almeida Theater are known for their creative creations and state of the art exhibitions. These personal spaces give a stage to new ability and exploratory works, adding to the region's dynamic theatre scene.

Social Tourist spots and Attractions

Past its theaters, the West End is home to various social milestones and attractions. Trafalgar Square, with its transcending Nelson's Segment and the Public Display, is a point of convergence of the area. The Public Exhibition houses a broad assortment of Western European artistic creations, including works by bosses like Van Gogh, Da Vinci, and Rembrandt.

Covent Nursery, when a clamoring market, is currently a dynamic center of road entertainers, store shops, and connoisseur eateries. The Imperial Drama House, situated in Covent Nursery, offers elite show and expressive dance exhibitions, proceeding with its heritage as a chief social organization.

The English Exhibition hall, found simply a short stroll from the core of the West End, is another must-visit objective. With curios traversing more than 2,000,000 years of history, including the Rosetta Stone and the Elgin Marbles, it gives an interesting look into the world's social legacy.

Shopping and Nightlife

The West End is likewise a head shopping location, with notorious roads like Oxford Road, Official Road, and Bond Road offering everything from high-road style to extravagance brands. Retail chains, for example, Selfridges and Freedom are milestones by their own doing, joining memorable design with current retail encounters.

As dusks, the West End changes into a clamoring nightlife center point. Soho, known for its diverse blend of bars, clubs, and eateries, offers something for each taste. Whether you're in the state of mind for a calm beverage in a customary bar or an evening of moving in a trendy club, Soho conveys.

The Contemporary West End

In contemporary times, the West End keeps on advancing, blending its rich legacy with current advancement. New theaters and execution spaces are persistently being created, guaranteeing that the region stays at the very front of worldwide amusement. The yearly Olivier Grants, commending the best in English theater, feature the West End's job as a forerunner in the performing expressions.

The locale's capacity to draw in top ability from around the world guarantees a different and excellent cluster of creations. From exemplary restorations to historic new works, the West End offers a venue experience that is unrivalled.

South Bank

The South Bank of the Thames Waterway, extending from Westminster Extension to Pinnacle Scaffold, is quite possibly of London's most dynamic and various region. Famous for its social tourist spots, clamoring expressions scene, and beautiful perspectives, the South Bank offers an unmatched encounter for the two local people and guests. This exposition dives into the appeal of South Bank, featuring its key attractions, authentic importance, and special climate.

A Social Focal point

South Bank is inseparable from culture and inventiveness. It is home to a portion of London's most notorious social organisations, which all in all add to the area's dynamic and vivacious person.

The Southbank Center, a rambling expressions complex, is at the core of the area. It incorporates the Imperial Celebration Corridor, the Hayward Display, and the Sovereign Elizabeth Lobby, offering a rich program of music, dance, visual expressions, and writing. The Southbank Center hosts significant occasions like the London Writing Celebration and the Implosion Celebration, drawing in specialists and crowds from around the globe.

Contiguous to the Southbank Center is the Public Theater, a main scene for elite show and execution. The theatre's three amphitheatres feature a variety of creations, from exemplary plays to contemporary works. Its riverside area likewise offers shocking perspectives on the city horizon, giving a beautiful setting to a night of theater.

The BFI Southbank, another social diamond, is the English Film Establishment's lead setting. It is a safe house for film fans, offering screenings of exemplary movies, contemporary film, and extraordinary occasions, for example, the BFI

London Film Celebration. The Mediatheque, housed inside the BFI, gives free admittance to a huge chronicle of English film and TV, permitting guests to dive into the country's true to life history.

Verifiable Importance

South Bank's set of experiences is basically as rich as its social contributions. By and large, this region was a center for diversion and trade. In the Elizabethan period, it was known for its theaters, including Shakespeare's Globe. The cutting edge Shakespeare's Globe, a remaking of the first, keeps on praising the Poet's heritage with credible creations and instructive projects.

The London Prison offers a more shocking look into the city's past, with intuitive shows and live entertainers rejuvenating the hazier parts of London's set of experiences. Close by, the Supreme Conflict Historical center South is housed in the previous Bethlem Imperial Medical clinic and presents a piercing investigation of war and its effect on society.

Grand Magnificence and Recreation

South Bank's grand magnificence and recreation valuable open doors make it a most loved spot for unwinding and diversion. The Thames Way, a riverside walkway, offers breathtaking perspectives on the waterway and tourist spots like the Places of Parliament, St. Paul's House of God, and the Pinnacle Scaffold. The way is ideally suited for a comfortable walk, an energetic run, or a serene bicycle ride.

The London Eye, a notorious Ferris wheel, gives an unmatched vantage highlight take in the city's horizon. A ride on the Eye offers all encompassing perspectives that stretch for a significant distance, making it a must-visit fascination for first-time guests and local people the same.

For those looking for a more serene encounter, the Celebration Nurseries and Bernie Spain Nurseries offer green spaces to loosen up and partake in the outside. These parks give a quiet retreat in the midst of the hurrying around of the city, with flawlessly finished regions ideal for picnics and unwinding.

Gastronomic Joys

South Bank's culinary scene is essentially as different as its social contributions. The region brags and exhibits feasting choices, from easygoing road food to high end food. The Southbank Center Food Market is a foodie's heaven, offering different worldwide cooking styles and distinctive items. Whether you're in the temperament for connoisseur burgers, valid paella, or newly heated baked goods, the market takes care of all preferences.

For a more upscale eating experience, eateries like Skylon and OXO Pinnacle Eatery offer dazzling dinners with staggering perspectives on the Thames. These foundations give the ideal setting for a unique evening out on the town, joining culinary greatness with stunning landscapes.

East London

East London, once overshadowed by the grandeur of central London, has emerged as a dynamic and vibrant area that embodies the spirit of modern urban transformation. From its rich history and diverse cultural scene to its innovative enterprises and eclectic neighborhoods, East London offers a unique and compelling experience for residents and visitors alike. This essay delves into the multifaceted appeal of East London and why it has become a must-visit destination.

Historical Roots and Cultural Heritage

East London's history is deeply intertwined with the industrial and maritime heritage of the city. The area played a crucial role during the Industrial Revolution, with the docks along the River Thames serving as a hub for global trade. The Museum of London Docklands, housed in a converted 19th-century warehouse, vividly chronicles this era, showcasing artifacts and stories from the time when the East End was the heart of London's trading empire.

Walking through the streets of East London, one can encounter remnants of its storied past. The historic district of Spitalfields, once a refuge for Huguenot silk weavers, retains its 18th-century charm with beautifully preserved Georgian houses and the iconic Spitalfields Market. Nearby, Brick Lane's vibrant street art and markets reflect the area's rich cultural mosaic, shaped by waves of immigration from Jewish, Bangladeshi, and other communities.

A Melting Pot of Cultures

East London is renowned for its cultural diversity. This melting pot of traditions is evident in the myriad of festivals, food markets, and cultural institutions that dot the area. The annual Brick Lane Curry Festival celebrates the neighborhood's Bangladeshi heritage, while the East End Film Festival showcases the talents of local and international filmmakers.

The culinary scene in East London is a testament to its multicultural fabric. From the tantalizing flavors of Brick Lane's curry houses to the trendy eateries of Shoreditch, food enthusiasts can embark on a global culinary journey without leaving the area. The famous Columbia Road Flower Market, held every Sunday, not only offers a riot of colors and scents but also reflects the community spirit and eclectic nature of East London.

Artistic Innovation and Creative Hubs

East London has become synonymous with creativity and innovation. Shoreditch, often considered the epicenter of this transformation, boasts an array of art galleries, design studios, and tech startups. The streets are adorned with ever-changing murals and street art, making the neighborhood an open-air gallery that attracts artists from around the world.

The area's creative energy is further fueled by venues like the Old Truman Brewery, a former brewery now home to artists' studios, independent shops, and event spaces. The Whitechapel Gallery, an institution since 1901, continues to champion contemporary art, hosting exhibitions that push boundaries and provoke thought.

Tech and Innovation

East London's transformation into a technology and innovation hub is epitomized by the rise of Tech City, also known as Silicon Roundabout, in Shoreditch. This cluster of tech companies, startups, and co-working spaces has positioned East London as a major player in the global tech scene. The area's dynamic ecosystem fosters collaboration and entrepreneurship, attracting talent from around the world.

Innovation extends beyond technology, with initiatives like the East London Fashion Cluster supporting emerging designers and sustainable fashion practices. This blend of tradition and forward-thinking makes East London a breeding ground for new ideas and trends.

Green Spaces and Community Spirit

Despite its urban hustle, East London offers pockets of tranquility and green spaces. Victoria Park, known as the "People's Park," provides a lush escape with its boating lake, gardens, and sports facilities. The park hosts numerous events and festivals, creating a vibrant community hub.

Further east, the Queen Elizabeth Olympic Park, developed for the 2012 London Olympics, has transformed into a sprawling public space with recreational facilities, walking trails, and cultural venues. The park symbolizes the area's regeneration and commitment to sustainable urban living.

North London

North London, a region frequently eclipsed by its southern partner, is a dynamic embroidery of history, culture, and natural beauty. From the varied areas and noteworthy landmarks to the lavish green spaces and flourishing expressions scene, North London offers an encounter that is both improving and charming. This exposition investigates why North London is a must-visit objective for anybody hoping to encounter the genuine embodiment of the city.

Historical Depth and Architectural Marvels

North London flaunts a rich history that is reflected in its different engineering and notable destinations. One of the most notable landmarks is Alexandra Royal residence, tenderly known as "Partner Pally." Initially opened in 1873 as a public community for diversion, schooling, and amusement, it keeps on facilitating various occasions, including shows, presentations, and ice skating. The all encompassing perspectives on London from its ridge area are basically stunning.

Hampstead, with its interesting town air, is one more gem of North London. Hampstead Heath, a huge and old parkland, offers an ideal getaway from the metropolitan hustle. The region is specked with notable structures, like Kenwood House, a neoclassical estate that houses a sublime craftsmanship assortment. The winding roads and charming houses of Hampstead give guests a brief look into London's past.

Further east, the antiquated city of Highgate is home to the renowned Highgate Graveyard, where eminent figures like Karl Marx and George Eliot are covered. This graveyard isn't simply a resting place yet a Gothic wonder with its congested pathways and barometrical charm.

Cultural Hotspots and Artistic Flair

North London is a cultural safe house with a flourishing expressions scene that matches any area of the city. Camden Town, frequently thought to be the thumping heart of elective culture, is prestigious for its energetic business sectors, unrecorded music scenes, and road craftsmanship. Camden Market, with its varied blend of slows down, offers everything from one of a kind style to worldwide road food. The Roundhouse, a notable scene, has a variety of exhibitions from state of the art theater to top notch shows.

The area of Islington, with its exquisite Georgian condos, is a cultural area of interest with a plenty of theaters, displays, and shops. The Almeida Theater and the Ruler's Head Theater are famous for their creative creations and close settings. Islington's Upper Road is fixed with bistros, eateries, and free shops, making it a wonderful spot to investigate.

Green Spaces and Natural Beauty

North London is honored with a wealth of green spaces that give a quiet break from city life. Hampstead Heath, referenced prior, is a rambling park with woodlands, knolls, and lakes. It is a famous spot for swimming, picnicking, and partaking in the stunning perspectives from Parliament Slope.

Official's Park, one of the Regal Parks of London, offers perfectly manicured gardens, a drifting lake, and the prestigious London Zoo. The recreation area's Outdoors Theater has exhibitions all through the late spring, giving a mystical encounter under the stars.

Finsbury Park, another critical green space, is a center point of sporting exercises, from sailing and tennis to live concerts. The recreation area's tranquil climate and grand beauty make it a #1 among locals and guests the same.

Culinary Delights and Shopping Experiences

North London's culinary scene is basically as different as its populace. From very good quality eateries to comfortable bistros and clamoring road markets, there is something to fulfill each sense of taste. In Camden, guests can enjoy various worldwide cooking styles, from credible Thai road food to customary English charge.

Islington's feasting scene is similarly great, with a scope of choices from Michelin-featured cafés to charming bistros. The region's food markets, for example, Exmouth Market, offer a variety of new produce and connoisseur delights.

For shopping devotees, North London doesn't frustrate. Camden Market is a gold mine of one of a kind finds, from classic dress to handmade specialties. Islington's Church Market offers a more customary shopping experience, with slows down selling new produce, dress, and family merchandise.

Community Spirit and Local Charm

What genuinely separates North London is areas of strength for its of community and local charm. Every area has its unmistakable person and energy, adding to the area's rich cultural mosaic. The well disposed locals, free organizations, and community occasions make an inviting environment that causes guests to feel at ease.

From the artistic spirit of Camden to the memorable tastefulness of Hampstead and the energetic energy of Islington, North London epitomizes the variety and dynamism of the capital city. Its mix of history, culture, natural beauty, and community spirit makes it a location that offers both energy and serenity.

A Geographical Picture of North London

West London

West London, a locale eminent for its affluence, noteworthy landmarks, and vibrant cultural scene, presents a captivating mix of old-world charm and contemporary sophistication. From the rich neighborhoods of Kensington and Chelsea to the clamoring markets of Notting Hill, West London offers an array of encounters that cater to the two occupants and guests. This essay digs into the interesting aspects that make West London an alluring destination.

A Stroll Through Opulence

West London is inseparable from extravagance and elegance, exemplified by areas like Kensington and Chelsea. These areas are home to dazzling Georgian and Victorian architecture, tree-lined roads, and probably the most costly real estate on the planet. The Royal Ward of Kensington and Chelsea boasts notorious landmarks like Kensington Palace, the official home of several individuals from the English royal family. The palace, set inside the peaceful Kensington Gardens, offers a brief look into royal history with its perfect State Apartments and rich gardens.

Simply not far off, the Victoria and Albert Gallery, the Natural History Historical center, and the Science Exhibition hall stand as pillars of cultural and educational improvement. These organizations house vast assortments of art, artifacts, and shows that span hundreds of years, making them must-visit destinations for history and art enthusiasts.

The Vibrant Pulse of Notting Hill

Notting Hill, one of West London's most notorious locale, is famous for its annual Notting Hill Carnival, a celebration of Caribbean culture that attracts a great many guests. The carnival, with its vibrant parades, music, and dance, transforms the roads into an uproar of variety and energy. Be that as it may, Notting Hill's charm stretches out past this merry occasion. The area is known for its pastel-shaded houses, quaint cafes, and the clamoring Portobello Road Market. This market, one of the world's largest antiques markets, offers everything from vintage attire and extraordinary collectibles to new deliver and connoisseur road food.

The area's bohemian energy is further enhanced by its free shops, art galleries, and mixed restaurants, making it a hub for creatives and innovators. The Electric Cinema, perhaps of the most established working cinema in the UK, gives a dash of old-world glamor with its extravagant seating and vintage stylistic layout, offering an extraordinary film going experience.

Cultural Richness and Entertainment

West London is a cultural area of interest, home to various theaters, music settings, and artistic establishments. The Royal Albert Hall, an undeniably popular show hall in Kensington, has a different array of performances, from classical shows and rock gigs to ballet and opera. The Verse Hammersmith, a leading theater in Hammersmith, is known for its innovative creations and obligation to sustaining new talent.

For music darlings, the Shepherd's Shrubbery Domain and the Hammersmith Apollo are notorious scenes that have facilitated legendary artists and keep on being key stops for international visits. These scenes, saturated with musical history, offer an intimate setting to appreciate live performances from many types.

Green Spaces and Tranquility

In spite of its urban sophistication, West London offers ample green spaces for relaxation and recreation. Hyde Park, one of London's largest and most famous parks, gives a tranquil oasis amidst the city's hurrying around. Guests can appreciate boating on the Serpentine Lake, horseback riding, or basically strolling through the beautifully landscaped gardens.

Holland Park, another jewel, is known for its Kyoto Garden, a tranquil Japanese garden total with koi lakes and waterfalls. This park also features an outdoors theater and various brandishing facilities, making it a favorite spot for both relaxation and activity.

Culinary Delights

West London's culinary scene is as different as its population. From Michelin-starred restaurants to charming road food stalls, the area offers a gastronomic adventure for each palate. The Ledbury in Notting Hill, with its innovative cooking and impeccable help, is a favorite among food experts. Meanwhile, the multicultural impact is obvious in the variety of eateries offering global cooking styles, from Indian and Center Eastern to Italian and Japanese.

For a quintessentially English encounter, afternoon tea at The Orangery in Kensington Palace or The Achievement Lodging is a wonderful guilty pleasure. These scenes offer an elegant setting to partake in a choice of finely fermented teas, finger sandwiches, and impeccable pastries.

A Hub of Innovation and Business

West London isn't simply a haven of culture and relaxation; it is also a flourishing business hub. Areas, for example, Hammersmith and Chiswick are home to various corporate headquarters and media companies, contributing significantly to the local economy. The area's strategic location, with astounding transport connections and nearness to Heathrow Airport, makes it an attractive base for businesses and professionals.

A geographical picture of west London

Types of Accommodation

Finding the right place to stay is a crucial part of planning any trip, and London, with its vast array of options, can be both exciting and overwhelming. Whether you're visiting for a short holiday, a business trip, or a longer stay, understanding the different types of accommodation available in London will help you make the best choice for your needs and budget.

Hotels

Hotels are the most common type of accommodation and range from luxurious five-star establishments to budget-friendly options.

   1.   **Luxury Hotels:** These offer top-notch services and amenities such as spas, fine dining restaurants, and concierge services. Examples include The Ritz, The Savoy, and The Dorchester. They are usually located in central areas like Mayfair, Knightsbridge, and Westminster.

   2.   **Mid-range Hotels:** These provide comfortable accommodations without the high price tag of luxury hotels. They often include amenities like free Wi-Fi, breakfast, and fitness centers.

Popular chains like Premier Inn and Holiday Inn fall into this category.

3. **Budget Hotels:** For travelers looking to save money, budget hotels like Travelodge and Ibis offer basic yet comfortable rooms. They might not have many frills, but they are clean, convenient, and often located near public transportation.

Bed and Breakfasts (B&Bs)

Bed and Breakfasts offer a more personal touch compared to hotels. Typically, they are small, family-run establishments where guests can stay in a cozy room and enjoy a home-cooked breakfast in the morning. B&Bs are found throughout London, often in quieter residential areas, giving guests a taste of local life.

Hostels

Hostels are an excellent choice for budget-conscious travelers, especially young backpackers and solo travelers. They offer dormitory-style rooms with shared bathrooms and communal kitchens. Some hostels also provide private rooms. Notable hostels in London include YHA London Central and Clink78. Hostels are great for meeting other travelers and often organize social activities.

Serviced Apartments

Serviced apartments combine the comfort of a hotel with the independence of having your own place. They come with fully equipped kitchens, living areas, and often, housekeeping services. This type of accommodation is ideal for families, groups, or anyone planning an extended stay. Examples include Citadines Apart'hotels and Fraser Suites.

Vacation Rentals

Vacation rentals, such as those listed on Airbnb, offer a wide variety of options, from entire homes to private rooms in someone's house. This type of accommodation allows you to live like a local and often provides more space and privacy than a hotel. It's perfect for families, groups, or those who prefer a homey atmosphere.

Boutique Hotels

Boutique hotels are smaller, stylish hotels that offer a unique and intimate experience. Each boutique hotel has its own distinct character and charm, often themed or with a focus on personalized service. They are scattered throughout trendy neighborhoods like Shoreditch, Notting Hill, and Covent Garden.

Guesthouses

Guesthouses are similar to B&Bs but might not include breakfast. They are usually small, family-owned establishments offering a few rooms to guests. They provide a comfortable and affordable option with a personal touch.

Student Accommodation

For longer stays, such as studying abroad, student accommodation is a practical option. Universities often offer dormitory-style housing, but there are also private student accommodations like Unite Students and Chapter Living, which provide rooms with shared or private facilities, common areas, and organized events.

Houseboats

For a truly unique experience, consider staying on a houseboat. Moored along the canals in areas like Little Venice and the River Thames, houseboats offer a cozy and charming place to stay. They provide all the basic amenities and the unique experience of living on the water.

Capsule Hotels

A relatively new concept in London, capsule hotels provide small, pod-like rooms that are perfect for travelers needing just a place to sleep. They are highly efficient and often located near major transport hubs. Capsule hotels like YOTELAIR at Heathrow and Gatwick airports are convenient for short layovers.

Chapter 5: Top Attractions

London is one of the most exciting cities in the world, offering a mix of history, culture, and modern attractions that appeal to visitors of all ages. Whether you're a history buff, an art lover, or just looking for some fun, London has something for everyone. Here are some of the top attractions you won't want to miss.

1. The British Museum

The British Museum is a treasure trove of human history and culture, showcasing artifacts from all over the world. It's home to the famous Rosetta Stone, which helped decipher Egyptian hieroglyphs, and the Elgin Marbles, originally part of the Parthenon in Athens. Best of all, entry to the museum is free, making it an accessible option for everyone.

2. The Tower of London

The Tower of London is a historic castle on the banks of the River Thames. Built by William the Conqueror in 1066, it has served as a royal palace, a prison, and even a zoo. Today, it's best known for housing the Crown Jewels, a dazzling collection of royal regalia. The Beefeaters, or Yeoman Warders, provide entertaining and informative tours that bring the Tower's history to life.

3. Buckingham Palace

No visit to London is complete without seeing Buckingham Palace, the official residence of the British monarch. While the palace itself is only open to the public during the summer months, you can watch the Changing of the Guard ceremony, which takes place daily from April to July and every other day for the rest of the year. It's a colorful display of British pageantry that's free to watch.

4. The Houses of Parliament and Big Ben

The Houses of Parliament, also known as the Palace of Westminster, is a stunning example of Gothic architecture and home to the UK's government. Big Ben, the iconic clock tower, is part of this complex. While Big Ben is currently undergoing renovations, the sight of the majestic buildings along the Thames is still impressive. You can also take a guided tour inside to learn about British politics and history.

5. The London Eye

For a bird's-eye view of the city, head to the London Eye, a giant Ferris wheel located on the South Bank of the River Thames. The ride takes about 30 minutes and offers breathtaking views of London's skyline, including the Houses of Parliament, St. Paul's Cathedral, and the Shard. It's a great way to get your bearings and see the city from a new perspective.

6. The Tate Modern

Art enthusiasts will love the Tate Modern, housed in a former power station on the banks of the Thames. It's one of the world's leading contemporary art museums, featuring works by Picasso, Warhol, and Hockney, among others. Admission is free, though special exhibitions may require a ticket.

7. The Natural History Museum

The Natural History Museum is a favorite for families, offering fascinating exhibits on everything from dinosaurs to human biology. The grand entrance hall is dominated by a giant blue whale skeleton, and there are plenty of interactive displays to engage visitors of all ages. Entry is free, making it an excellent option for a budget-friendly day out.

8. Covent Garden

Covent Garden is a bustling area known for its shopping, dining, and entertainment. Street performers, or "buskers," provide free shows, ranging from magic tricks to acrobatics. The historic market building houses a variety of shops and restaurants, and nearby theatres offer world-class performances, including many popular West End shows.

9. Hyde Park

Hyde Park is one of London's largest and most famous parks, offering a green oasis in the heart of the city. It's a great place to relax, have a picnic, or go for a leisurely stroll. Highlights include the Serpentine Lake, where you can rent a paddleboat, and Speaker's Corner, a traditional spot for public debates and speeches.

10. The Shard

For another spectacular view of London, visit The Shard, the tallest building in the UK. The observation deck, known as The View from The Shard, is on the 72nd floor and offers 360-degree views of the city. On a clear day, you can see for up to 40 miles in every direction. It's a bit pricey, but the experience is unforgettable.

The Tower of London

Buckingham Palace

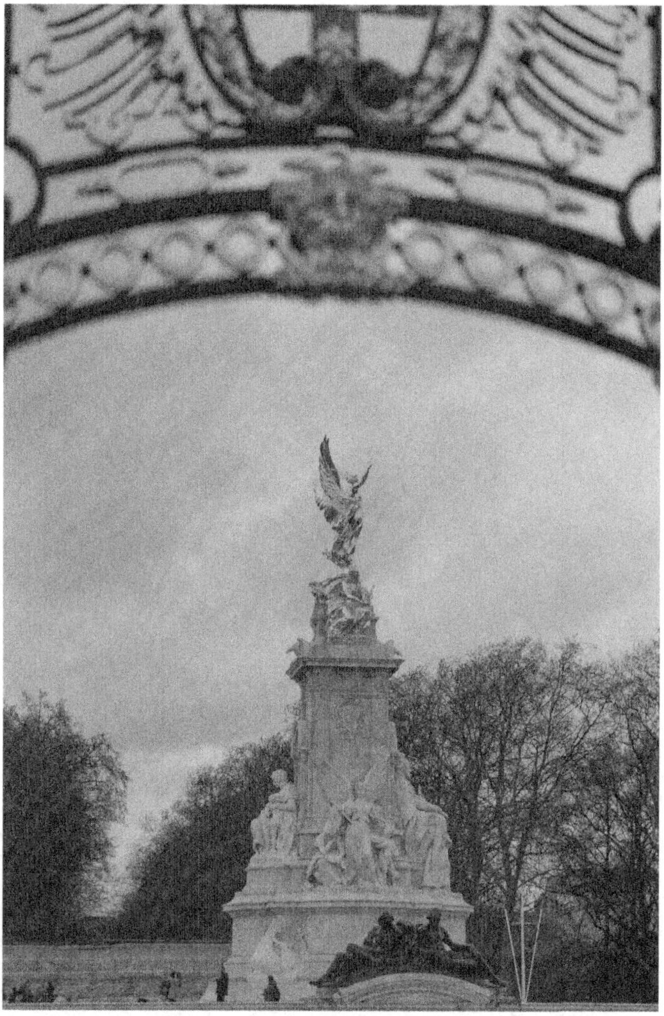

Westminster Abbey

Houses of Parliament and Big Ben

Museums and Galleries

The British Museum

National Gallery

Tate Modern

Natural History Museum

Parks and Gardens

London, quite possibly of the most active city on the planet, is likewise home to the absolute most lovely stops and gardens. These green spaces give a tranquil break from the rushing about of metropolitan life. Whether you're a neighborhood or a vacationer, investigating London's parks and gardens is an unquestionable necessity. This paper will direct you through probably the most well known and beautiful green spaces in the city.

Hyde Park

Hyde Park is one of the biggest and most well known parks in London. Situated in the core of the city, it covers 350 sections of land and offers a large number of exercises. You can lease a paddleboat and partake in a comfortable ride on the Serpentine Lake, or basically loosen up on the grass with a decent book. The recreation area is likewise home to the Diana, Princess of Ribs Remembrance Wellspring, a wonderful and peaceful spot to reflect and loosen up. Hyde Park has numerous occasions and shows, making it an energetic spot to visit consistently.

Regent's Park

Regent's Park, situated in the northwestern piece of London, is another pearl. This park is known for its shocking gardens and open spaces. The Sovereign Mary's Gardens inside Regent's Park are especially popular for their delightful rose gardens, including north of 12,000 roses of various assortments. The recreation area likewise has a drifting lake, sports offices, and the renowned ZSL London Zoo. Whether you're keen on a serene walk or a pleasant outing with family, Regent's Park brings something to the table.

St. James' Park

St. James' Park is the most established Illustrious Park in London, arranged before Buckingham Royal residence. This park is ideal for a relaxed stroll, with its beautiful perspectives on the castle and the lake. The recreation area is home to an assortment of natural life, including pelicans, which were first acquainted with the recreation area as a gift from the Russian representative in 1664. The recreation area likewise offers superb perspectives on the Pony Watchmen March and the London Eye. With its focal area and noteworthy importance, St. James' Park is a #1 among the two local people and vacationers.

Kensington Gardens

Kensington Gardens, when the confidential gardens of Kensington Royal residence, is presently a recreational area that holds a glorious appeal. The recreation area is home to a few eminent attractions, including the Serpentine Exhibitions, the Albert Commemoration, and the Peter Skillet sculpture. The Italian Gardens, a lovely 150-year-old fancy water garden, is a tranquil spot inside the recreation area. Kensington Gardens consistently associates with Hyde Park, offering guests a broad green space to investigate.

Green Park

Green Park is a quiet space situated between Hyde Park and St. James' Park. Dissimilar to different parks, it has no lakes or structures, simply completely open glades and mature trees. This straightforwardness gives Green Park a one of a kind appeal. It's an extraordinary spot for an excursion or a peaceful rest in the shade. During spring, the recreation area is covered with a wonderful rug of daffodils, making it a magnificent spot to visit.

Victoria Park

Situated in East London, Victoria Park is frequently alluded to as "Individuals' Park." It's a #1 among local people for its local area occasions and sporting exercises. The recreation area has two huge lakes, a drifting lake, and a jungle gym, making it an optimal spot for families. Victoria Park likewise has live events and open air films, uniting the local area in an energetic air.

Kew Gardens

The Regal Botanic Gardens, Kew, generally known as Kew Gardens, is a widely acclaimed greenhouse in southwest London. Crossing more than 300 sections of land, Kew Gardens is home to the biggest and most different assortment of plants on the planet. Guests can investigate the lovely glasshouses, for example, the Palm House and the Calm House, which house an immense range of fascinating plants. The Treetop Walkway offers an exceptional viewpoint, permitting guests to stroll among the treetops and appreciate shocking perspectives on the gardens. Kew Gardens is an UNESCO World Legacy Site and a must-visit for plant lovers.

Richmond Park

Richmond Park, situated in southwest London, is the biggest of the Regal Parks. Covering more than 2,500 sections of land, it's a sanctuary for natural life, including crowds of deer that wander openly. The recreation area offers different scenes, from open meadows to lush regions, making it an ideal spot for climbing, cycling, and picnicking. The Isabella Estate, a forest nursery inside the recreation area, is especially gorgeous in the spring when the azaleas and rhododendrons are in blossom. Richmond Park gives a quiet retreat from the city, with shocking perspectives on the London horizon from the highest point of Lord Henry's Hill.

Hyde Park

Kew Gardens

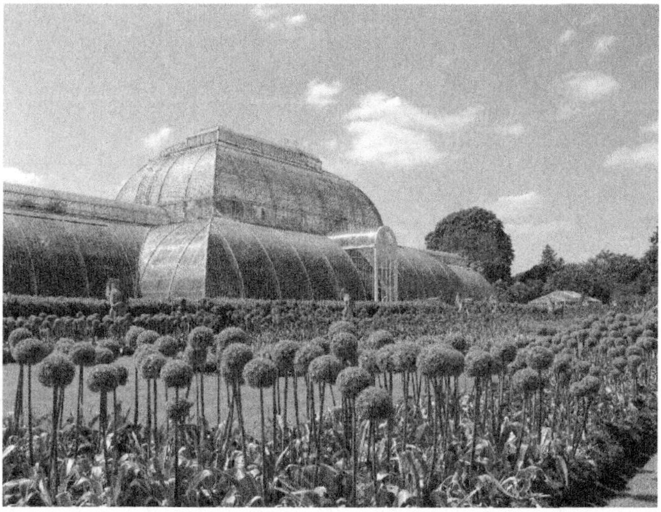

Regent's Park

Hampstead Heath

Modern Attractions

London is a city that delightfully mixes its rich verifiable past with state of the art modernity. While the city is prestigious for its famous milestones like the Pinnacle of London and Buckingham Castle, it additionally brags a plenty contemporary attractions that take special care of all interests. This exposition investigates a portion of the must-visit modern attractions in London, exhibiting the city's lively, dynamic, and imaginative soul.

The Shard

Standing tall as the tallest structure in the UK, The Shard is a wonder of modern engineering. Its smooth, glass configuration is a striking element of London's skyline. Guests can take a lift to The View from The Shard, situated on the 72nd floor, where they are blessed to receive stunning 360-degree perspectives on the city. On a crisp morning, you can see up to 40 miles toward each path. The Shard likewise houses a few very good quality cafés and a lavish inn, making it a multi-layered objective.

The London Eye

The London Eye is another notable modern fascination that offers marvelous perspectives on the city. This goliath Ferris wheel, arranged on the South Bank of the Thames, stands 135 meters tall. Every one of its glass containers gives an unmatched vantage highlight seeing milestones like Huge Ben, St. Paul's Cathedral, and the Places of Parliament. The 30-minute ride is both invigorating and tranquil, giving a remarkable method for valuing London's magnificence.

The Tate Modern

Workmanship lovers will track down a shelter at the Tate Modern, housed in the previous Bankside Power Station. This undeniably popular display grandstands contemporary and modern craftsmanship from around the globe. With works by specialists like Picasso, Warhol, and Hockney, the Tate Modern expresses a different and viewpoint inciting assortment. The actual structure is a compositional jewel, with a strikingly modern plan that stands out delightfully from its modern past. The display likewise includes intelligent shows and a dazzling perspective on the Thames from its highest level eatery.

The Sky Garden

For the individuals who love all encompassing perspectives however incline toward a more loosened up climate, the Sky Garden is an optimal objective. Situated at the highest point of the "Walkie-Talkie" constructing, the Sky Garden is an interesting public space highlighting rich gardens, perception decks, and outdoors patios. Affirmation is free, yet it's fitting to book ahead of time because of its prominence. The Sky Garden offers a peaceful break from the rushing about of the city underneath, with the special reward of staggering cityscapes.

The Science Museum

The Science Museum in South Kensington is a captivating objective for guests, everything being equal. With intelligent shows that cover all that from space investigation to state of the art innovation, the museum is both instructive and engaging. Features incorporate the Apollo 10 order module, a VR spacewalk insight, and the Wonderlab, an intelligent exhibition intended to motivate youthful personalities. The museum additionally has impermanent presentations, so there's continuously a novel, new thing to find.

The O2 Arena

The O2 Arena is London's head diversion setting, facilitating shows, games, and displays. This huge vault molded structure, initially worked for the thousand years festivities, has been changed into a center of movement. From undeniably popular performers to exciting games coordinates, the O2 offers an extensive variety of diversion choices. Moreover, the encompassing region, known as the O2 Diversion Road, includes different eateries, bars, and, surprisingly, a film, making it an extraordinary spot to go through a whole night.

Camden Market

For a more mixed and lively experience, Camden Market is a must-visit. Situated in the enthusiastic Camden Town, this market is well known for its elective design, remarkable artworks, and different road food. It's a social mixture where you can find everything from one of a kind dress to high quality gems and worldwide cooking. The market's enthusiastic environment is upgraded by road entertainers and unrecorded music, making it a tomfoolery and vivacious spot to investigate.

Covent Garden

Covent Garden is another incredible modern fascination that offers a blend of shopping, eating, and diversion. The noteworthy market constructing now houses popular shops, high quality food slows down, and jazzy eateries. Road entertainers add to the dynamic climate, engaging guests with their noteworthy demonstrations. Covent Garden is additionally home to the Imperial Show House, where you can get a-list exhibitions of drama and artful dance.

The Shard

London Eye

Millennium Bridge

The O2

Chapter 6: Culture and Entertainment

London, one of the world's most interesting urban communities, is a place where culture and entertainment are at the heart of everyday life. With a blend of history, variety, and innovation, London offers a wealth of cultural encounters and fun activities for individuals of all ages and interests. This essay investigates the rich cultural landscape and the myriad of entertainment choices that make London a must-visit destination.

A Melting Pot of Cultures

London is a city of unbelievable variety. Individuals from everywhere the world live and work here, bringing their one of a kind traditions, languages, and cooking styles. This melting pot of cultures is apparent in each edge of the city. For instance, in areas like Block Lane, you can track down vibrant Bangladeshi people group, while Chinatown offers a taste of Asia with its restaurants, shops, and festivals.

This cultural variety is celebrated through various festivals and occasions over time. Notable occasions incorporate the Notting Slope Carnival, Europe's greatest street festival celebrating Caribbean culture, and the Chinese New Year celebrations in Chinatown, which feature dragon dances, lanterns, and scrumptious food.

Art and Museums

London is home to a portion of the world's best museums and art galleries, many of which offer free passage. The English Exhibition hall, for example, houses north of 8,000,000 works, including the Rosetta Stone and the Elgin Marbles. This exhibition hall allows guests to travel through time and investigate ancient civilizations from Egypt to Rome.

For art darlings, the National Gallery in Trafalgar Square is a must-visit. It houses an assortment of more than 2,300 paintings, including works by Van Gogh, Leonardo da Vinci, and Rembrandt. The Tate Present day, located in a changed over power station on the banks of the Thames, showcases contemporary art from around the world. Its special architecture and state of the art shows make it a fascinating place to investigate.

Theater and Music

London's West End is inseparable from elite theater. Often compared to New York's Broadway, the West End offers a dazzling array of shows, from immortal classics like "The Phantom of the Opera" and "Les Misérables" to present day hits like "Hamilton" and "Harry Potter and the Reviled Youngster." The Globe Theater, a faithful reproduction of Shakespeare's original playhouse, offers an authentic encounter of the Bard's work in an outdoors setting.

Music darlings will track down a lot to appreciate in London. The city boasts famous scenes like the Royal Albert Hall, known for its shocking architecture and various performances, from classical shows to shake gigs. The O2 Arena, quite possibly of the largest indoor arena on the planet, has shows by top international artists. For a more intimate setting, scenes like Ronnie Scott's Jazz Club in Soho offer unrecorded music in a comfortable atmosphere.

Street Performances and Markets

London's streets are alive with performances and markets that add to the city's charm. Covent Garden is famous for its street entertainers, who entertain guests including magic stunts to acrobatics. It's also home to a variety of shops, cafes, and the noteworthy Apple Market, which sells handmade crafts and antiques.

Camden Market, located in the stylish Camden Town area, is a paradise for those looking for one of a kind fashion, art, and food. With more than

1,000 shops and stalls, it offers everything from vintage dress to international street food. Ward Market, near London Extension, is a food sweetheart's dream, with stalls selling new produce, artisanal bread, cheddar, and an array of international dishes.

Cinemas and Comedy

For film buffs, London offers a range of cinemas, from grand historical theaters to present day multiplexes. The Electric Cinema in Notting Slope is quite possibly of the most established working cinema in the UK, offering a lavish film watching experience with extravagant seating and connoisseur snacks. The BFI Southbank, part of the English Film Foundation, screens classic and contemporary movies, has film festivals, and offers shrewd talks and occasions.

Comedy sweethearts will track down a lot to laugh about in London. The Comedy Store in Soho is one of the city's most famous comedy clubs, featuring stand-up shows and comedy performances by the absolute best comedians. Smaller scenes like the Highly confidential Comedy Club give an intimate setting where arising talents and established comedians alike perform to enthusiastic audiences.

Sports and Outdoor Activities

Sports play a major part in London's entertainment scene. Football fans can visit famous stadiums like Wembley and Emirates to watch exciting matches. Wimbledon, the undeniably popular tennis tournament, attracts fans from everywhere the globe each mid year. For the people who favor participating in sports, London offers various parks and recreational areas for activities like cycling, running, and boating.

London's parks are ideally suited for a relaxing day out. Hyde Park, perhaps of the largest park in the city, offers boating on the Serpentine Lake, horseback riding, and outdoors shows. Official's Park is home to the ZSL London Zoo and beautiful gardens. Greenwich Park, with its staggering perspectives on the Waterway Thames and the

Royal Observatory, gives an ideal spot for picnics and comfortable walks.

Theatres and Performances

London is famous for its energetic and various theater scene, offering something for everyone. From grand, noteworthy theaters to small, intimate scenes, the city is a paradise for anyone who loves live performances. We should investigate what makes London's theater scene so special and why it's a must-visit for anyone inspired by the arts.

A Rich History of Theater

London's theater history dates back many years. One of the most famous historical theaters is Shakespeare's Globe. Originally implicit 1599, the cutting edge reconstruction of the Globe allows audiences to encounter plays similarly as they were in Shakespeare's time. Watching a performance here resembles venturing back ever, with the outdoors construction and standing area for the audience, known as the "yard."

Theater Royal Drury Lane, which opened in 1663, is another iconic setting. Known for its grand architecture and long history, it has facilitated many famous plays and musicals throughout the long term. Attending a show here means partaking in a great performance as well as being part of a setting's rich past.

The West End: London's Theater Hub

At the point when individuals consider London theater, they often consider the West End. This area is similar to Broadway in New York and is home to many of the city's greatest and most popular shows. Here, you can find long-running musicals like "The Phantom of the Opera," "Les Misérables," and "The Lion Ruler."

The West End is also where you'll find many famous actors performing on stage. Large names from film and television often take jobs in West End productions, adding an extra layer of energy for theater-attendees.

A Variety of Performances

One of the best things about London's theater scene is the variety of performances available. There are classic plays, current dramas, comedies, and experimental works. For the individuals who love musicals, London offers a range of options from large-scale productions to new and innovative shows.

Small theaters and periphery settings, similar to the Donmar Warehouse and the Royal Court Theater, offer an alternate encounter from the large West End theaters. These settings often showcase new plays and state of the art performances. They are great places to see new to the scene talent and original works that you won't find anywhere else.

Family-Friendly Shows

London's theaters are not only for adults. There are many family-friendly shows that children will adore. Productions like "Matilda the Musical," based on Roald Dahl's darling book, and "Harry Potter and the Reviled Youngster," which continues the tale of Harry Potter, are popular with families. These shows offer magical encounters that captivate both youthful and old audiences.

Affordable and Accessible Theater

While some theater tickets can be costly, there are many ways to partake in London's theater scene on a spending plan. TKTS in Leicester Square offers limited tickets for same-day performances. Many theaters also have special deals, rush tickets, and lotteries for cheaper seats. A few scenes, similar to the National Theater, offer affordable estimating for their shows, making theater accessible to everyone.

Theater Festivals and Events

London has several theater festivals and events over time. The London International Festival of Theater (LIFT) brings innovative and provocative performances from around the world to the city. The annual West End LIVE occasion offers free performances from probably the most popular shows, providing individuals with a taste of the West End's offerings.

The Impact of Theater on London's Culture

Theater is a vital part of London's cultural fabric. It unites individuals, sparks conversations, and offers a shared encounter that is both entertaining and provocative. Whether you're watching a satire that makes you laugh until you cry or a drama that challenges your perspectives, theater has a novel way of connecting with its audience.

West End Shows

London's West End resembles the heartbeat of the city's entertainment scene, similar to Broadway in New York. It's where you can discover probably the best theater creations on the planet, attracting audiences from all over. Here's the reason catching a West End show ought to be on your London list of must-dos.

A Theater Lover's Paradise

The West End is packed with theaters, each facilitating a variety of shows that range from classic musicals and plays to present day hits and experimental performances. Probably the most famous shows you can see incorporate "Les Misérables," "The Phantom of the Opera," and "Hamilton." There's always something previously unheard-of to watch.

Something for Everyone

Regardless of what your taste, the West End has a show for you. Love enormous musical numbers? Attempt "The Lion Ruler" or "Mamma Mia!" Favor a holding drama or a laugh-out-boisterous satire? There are a lot of those as well. Families, couples, and solo travelers can all track down something to appreciate.

Top-Notch Performances

West End shows are known for their excellent. The actors, artists, dancers, and musicians are probably truly incredible. The sets, ensembles, and special impacts are in many cases spectacular, making each performance a visual treat. Regardless of whether you're not an enormous theater fan, you could end up amazed by the talent and effort on display.

A Full Night Out

Going to a West End show isn't just about the performance. The theaters are located in a vivacious part of London, full of restaurants, bars, and shops. Many individuals make a night of it, having supper before the show or beverages afterward. It's a fantastic way to encounter the buzz of London nightlife.

Affordable Options

While certain tickets can be costly, there are ways to see a show without breaking the bank. Many theaters offer limited tickets for last-minute appointments, matinee performances, or special deals. There are also ticket offices like TKTS in Leicester Square where you can track down great costs on the day of the show.

Shakespeare's Globe

Shakespeare's Globe in London is a special place where you can step back in time and experience the magic of William Shakespeare's plays similarly as quite a while back. Here's the reason visiting the Globe ought to be on your London daily agenda.

A Modern Recreation of History

Shakespeare's Globe is a modern remaking of the original Globe Theater, which was worked in 1599. The original theater was where many of Shakespeare's famous plays were performed, yet it was obliterated by a fire in 1613. The ebb and flow Globe, located near the Thames Stream, was opened in 1997 and is intended to be as near the original as conceivable.

Open-Air Theater

One of the unique features of Shakespeare's Globe is its open-air plan. The theater has no roof over the central yard where individuals stand to watch the plays. This arrangement provides you with a taste of what watching a play in Shakespeare's time was like. Performances proceed with rain or sparkle, so it's really smart to accordingly look at the weather and dress!

Authentic Performances

The Globe is known for its authentic performances of Shakespeare's plays. The actors use ensembles and props similar to those from the sixteenth 100 years, and the stage is intended to match the original as intently as conceivable. The emphasis is on rejuvenating Shakespeare's words such that feels consistent with his era.

A Unique Viewing Experience

At the Globe, you can decide to sit in the covered galleries around the sides or stand in the open yard before the stage. Standing tickets are usually the cheapest and offer a nearby perspective on the action. This arrangement creates an energetic and interactive atmosphere, as standing spectators, known as "groundlings," can often interact with the entertainers.

Educational Programs and Tours

In addition to watching a play, you can also take a directed visit through the theater. The tours give fascinating experiences into the history of the original Globe, the recreation cycle, and how plays were acted in Shakespeare's time. The Globe also offers various educational programs and studios for all ages, making it a great destination for families and school gatherings.

Music and Concerts

London is a global center point for music darlings, offering an inconceivable range of shows and music events. Whether you appreciate rock, pop, classical, or jazz, London has something to offer every music fan. Here's the reason you ought to encounter the music scene in London.

A Rich Musical History

London has a rich musical history that has shaped the world of music. It's the birthplace of legendary bands like The Beatles, The Drifters, and Sovereign. Walking through the roads of London, you can feel the history and impact of these musical giants everywhere, from famous recording studios to notable show venues.

World-Famous Venues

The city is home to the absolute most famous music venues in the world. The Royal Albert Hall, with its dazzling architecture, has everything from classical shows to shake performances. The O2 Arena, perhaps of the largest indoor arena in

Europe, features top international artists and bands. Smaller, notable venues like the Roundhouse and the 100 Club offer more intimate show encounters.

A Variety of Genres

London's music scene is amazingly different. You can catch a classical show at the Barbican, appreciate jazz at Ronnie Scott's, or dance the night away to electronic music at Fabric. Regardless of what classification you like, you'll track it down in London. The city's multicultural makeup also means you can find music from everywhere in the world, including reggae, hip-bounce, and Latin music.

Festivals and Events

London has various music festivals and events consistently. The English Mid year Festival in Hyde Park features large name artists in a beautiful outside setting. The Notting Slope Carnival celebrates Caribbean music and culture with vibrant parades and live performances. There's always something happening in London's music scene, from free shows in parks to large-scale music festivals.

Live Music Every Night

Quite possibly the best thing about London is that there's live music every night. Bars and clubs across the city have local bands and anticipated artists, offering you the chance to find new talent. **Camden Town**, in particular, is famous for its live music venues and has a rich history of showcasing arising artists.

Royal Albert Hall

O2 Arena

Jazz Clubs

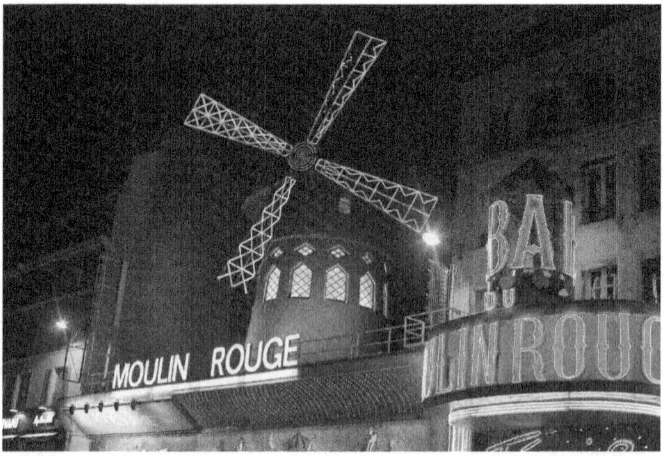
MOULIN ROUGE
BAL
DU
MOULIN ROUGE

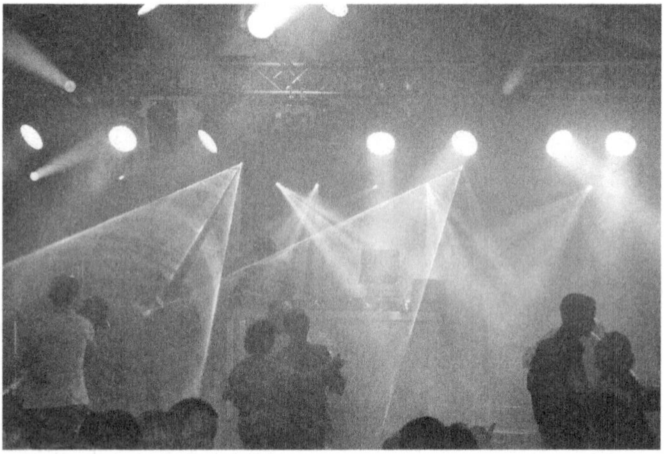

Art and Exhibitions

London is a treasure trove for art lovers. The city is packed with museums, galleries, and exhibitions that showcase a stunning variety of art from around the world. Whether you're a seasoned art enthusiast or just curious, London's art scene has something for everyone. Here's a quick guide to exploring art and exhibitions in London.

World-Class Museums and Galleries

London is home to some of the most famous museums and galleries in the world. The British Museum, for example, houses an incredible collection of artifacts from ancient civilizations, including the Rosetta Stone and Egyptian mummies. It's a fantastic place to learn about history and see amazing objects up close.

The National Gallery in Trafalgar Square is another must-visit. It features paintings from renowned artists like Van Gogh, Da Vinci, and Monet. Walking through its halls, you can see masterpieces that span centuries and styles.

Modern and Contemporary Art

If you're interested in modern and contemporary art, the Tate Modern is the place to go. Housed in a former power station, the Tate Modern showcases works from the 20th century to the present day. Its collection includes pieces by Picasso, Warhol, and Hockney. The building itself is a piece of art, with its industrial architecture and impressive views of the River Thames.

The Saatchi Gallery is another great spot for contemporary art. It focuses on young, emerging artists and often features bold and innovative works. It's a great place to discover new talent and see cutting-edge art.

Unique Exhibitions

London's art scene is always buzzing with special exhibitions. These temporary shows often focus on specific themes, artists, or periods. For example, you might find an exhibition dedicated to the works of a single artist, like a Picasso or Frida Kahlo show, or a themed exhibit exploring topics like fashion, photography, or digital art.

Many museums and galleries host these exhibitions, so there's always something new and exciting to see. It's worth checking the schedules of places like the Victoria and Albert Museum, the Design Museum, and the Royal Academy of Arts to see what's on during your visit.

Street Art and Public Installations

Art in London isn't confined to museums and galleries. The city is also famous for its street art. Areas like Shoreditch and Camden are known for their vibrant murals and graffiti. Walking through these neighborhoods, you can see colorful and thought-provoking works by artists like Banksy and local talent.

Public art installations are also common in London. Sculptures and art pieces are often displayed in parks, squares, and even along the river. These installations make art accessible to everyone and add to the city's creative vibe.

Accessible and Affordable

One of the best things about London's art scene is that many museums and galleries offer free admission to their permanent collections. This makes it easy for everyone to enjoy and appreciate art without worrying about the cost. Special exhibitions may have an entry fee, but there are often discounts and free days available.

Major Art Galleries

London is home to a portion of the world's best workmanship displays. These exhibitions offer a brief look into hundreds of years of imaginative accomplishment, displaying works from exemplary magnum opuses to contemporary manifestations. Here is a glance at a portion of the significant craftsmanship exhibitions you ought to visit in London.

The National Gallery

Situated in Trafalgar Square, the National Gallery is one of the most popular workmanship museums on the planet. It houses more than 2,300 compositions, going from the thirteenth 100 years to the mid twentieth hundred years. Here, you can see works by eminent craftsmen like Van Gogh, Da Vinci, and Rembrandt. The best part is that passage is free, making it open to everybody.

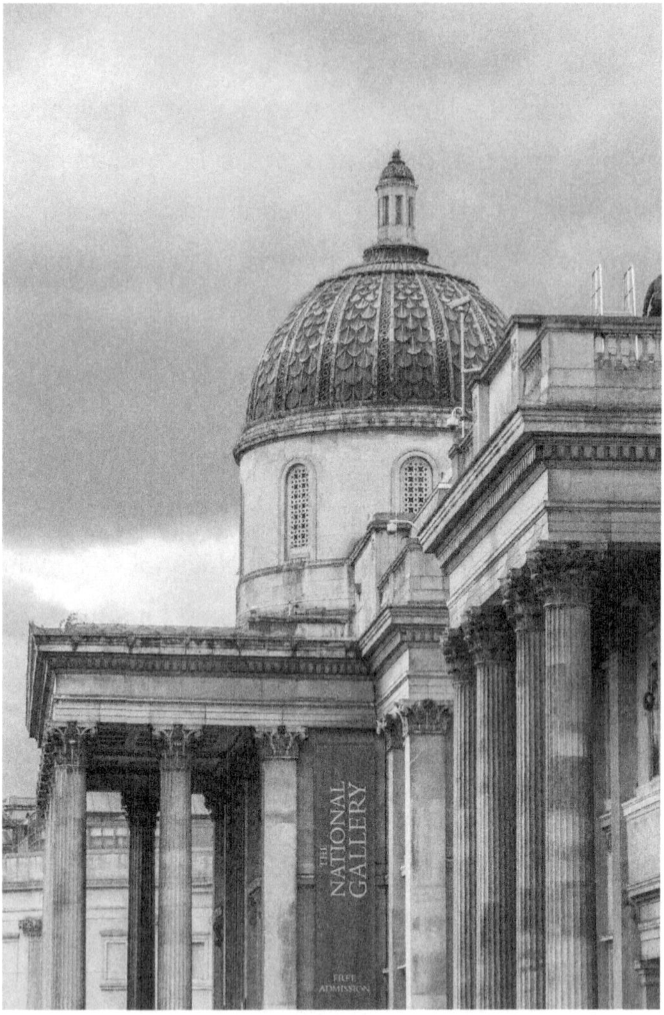
THE NATIONAL GALLERY
FREE ADMISSION

Tate Modern

In the event that you love modern and contemporary craftsmanship, Tate Modern is a must-visit. Arranged on the banks of the Thames in a previous power station, the gallery highlights works from the 1900s to the current day. You'll find pieces by craftsmen like Picasso, Warhol, and Hockney. The actual structure is a compositional wonder, offering staggering perspectives on the city from its porch.

Tate Britain

Tate Britain centres around English workmanship from the 1500s to the present. Situated in Millbank, it's home to a broad assortment of works by J.M.W. Turner, perhaps Britain's most popular painter. The gallery additionally includes pieces by other striking

English craftsmen like David Hockney and Lucian Freud. It's an incredible spot to investigate the rich history of English craftsmanship.

The Victoria and Albert Museum

Known as the V&A, the Victoria and Albert Museum in South Kensington is the world's biggest museum of ornamental expressions and plan. It houses everything from ceramics and style to models and artistic creations. The museum's mixed assortment traverses north of 5,000 years of workmanship, offering something for everybody. Features incorporate the Cast Courts and the broad assortment of Asian workmanship.

The Saatchi Gallery

For those keen on contemporary workmanship, the Saatchi Gallery in Chelsea is a top objective. Established by Charles Saatchi, the gallery exhibits state of the art works by arising craftsmen. The presentations frequently highlight provocative and intriguing pieces that push the limits of customary workmanship. It's a unique space where you can find very interesting abilities.

The Courtauld Gallery

Housed in the wonderful Somerset House, the Courtauld Gallery is prestigious for its great assortment of Impressionist and Post-Impressionist canvases. Here, you can see works of art by Monet, Degas, and Van Gogh, among others. The gallery is moderately little, making it simple to investigate and value the works of art at a relaxed speed.

Street Art Tours

London is famous for its rich history and culture, however did you know it's also a focal point for fantastic street art? Taking a street art tour in London is a fantastic way to investigate the city's creative side and see amazing artworks that you won't track down in historical centers.

What is Street Art?

Street art incorporates graffiti, murals, and other forms of public art created on structures, walls, and sidewalks. Dissimilar to traditional art found in galleries, street art is accessible to everybody and frequently mirrors the way of life and governmental issues of the city. London's street art scene is vibrant and consistently changing, with new pieces appearing regularly.

Popular Areas for Street Art

The absolute best places to see street art in London incorporate Shoreditch, Block Lane, and Camden. Shoreditch is known for its vivid murals and innovative plans. Block Lane is a clamoring area with art around each corner, including famous works by prestigious artists like Banksy. Camden, famous for its alternative culture, also boasts some unbelievable street art.

Why Take a Tour?

Taking a street art tour is a great way to learn more about the art and the artists behind it. Guides are usually knowledgeable locals who can share fascinating stories and experiences. They can call attention to unlikely treasures and explain the meanings behind the artworks. Additionally, tours frequently take you through cool neighborhoods you probably won't investigate otherwise.

The Artists

Many talented artists add to London's street art scene. Some, as Banksy, are famous overall for their provocative pieces. Others, as Stik and Ben Eine, have unique styles that make their work stand out. A tour can assist you with perceiving various artists and understand their impact on the art world.

A Unique Experience

Street art tours offer a unique and dynamic way to experience London. In contrast to traditional tours, where you could visit historic locales or exhibition halls, street art tours are constantly advancing as new artworks appear. It's a chance to see the city from a new point of view and appreciate the creativity that blossoms with its streets.

Festivals and Events

London is a city that loves to celebrate, and it has a wide assortment of festivals and events consistently. From music and food to cultural and seasonal festivals, there's continuously something energizing occurring. Here is a gander at probably the most well known festivals and events in London.

Music Festivals

London is an extraordinary spot for music darlings. The city has various music festivals including specialists from everywhere the world. One of the most popular is the English Late spring Celebration in Hyde Park, where enormous name bands and solo craftsmen act in the outdoors. Another well known occasion is the Remote Celebration, which centers around hip-jump, R&B, and grime music.

262

Food and Drink Festivals

For foodies, London offers a lot of delectable events. The Flavor of London celebration in Official's Park is a must-visit, with top culinary experts and eateries displaying their best dishes. You can test luxurious cuisine, watch cooking exhibitions, and even meet a portion of your number one culinary specialists. The London Mixed drink Week is another feature, where you can appreciate uniquely created mixed drinks at different bars across the city.

Cultural Festivals

London's assorted populace implies there are numerous cultural festivals celebrating various customs and legacies. The Notting Slope Amusement park is one of the biggest, observing Caribbean culture with energetic motorcades, music, and food. Chinese New Year in Chinatown is one more huge occasion, with winged serpent moves, lights, and tasty Chinese food.

Seasonal Events

Regardless of the season, there's continuously something merry occurring in London. In the colder time of year, Winter Wonderland in Hyde Park changes into an enchanted wonderland with ice skating, Christmas markets, and merry rides. In the late spring, the city wakes up with road fairs and outside exhibitions. One of the features is the City chairman's Thames Celebration, which highlights riverside exercises, firecrackers, and craftsmanship establishments.

Sporting Events

London is likewise a center for sports fans. The Wimbledon Tennis Titles draw fans from around the world to watch top tennis players contend. The London Long distance race is another significant occasion, where thousands of sprinters race through the city's roads, supported by energetic groups.

Christmas Markets

London wakes up during the Christmas season, and one of the most incredible ways of partaking in the festive soul is by visiting its Christmas markets. These markets are spread across the city and proposition a supernatural encounter for guests, everything being equal. Here's the reason you ought to look at them.

Festive Atmosphere

Christmas markets in London are loaded up with seasonal joy. They are wonderfully beautified with sparkling lights, festive garlands, and frequently highlight a monster Christmas tree. The air is loaded up with the fragrance of reflected on wine, simmered chestnuts, and gingerbread, making a comfortable and welcoming atmosphere.

Unique Gifts

In the event that you're searching for unique gifts, Christmas markets are the ideal spot. You'll find slows down selling handmade specialties, gems, adornments, and more. These things are many times stand-out and make for smart presents that you won't track down in customary stores.

Delicious Food and Drinks

The food at Christmas markets is a feature. You can partake in different treats, from customary German wieners and Belgian waffles to mince pies and hot cocoa. Many markets likewise offer reflected on wine, a warm, flavored drink that is ideal for cold winter nights.

Fun Activities

Christmas markets are not just about shopping and eating; they likewise offer a lot of fun activities. Many markets have ice skating arenas, where you can skim under the stars. Some have thrill rides, unrecorded music, and even St Nick's cave, where children can meet St Nick and offer their Christmas wishes.

Popular Markets

The absolute most popular Christmas markets in London remember Winter Wonderland for Hyde Park, Southbank Center Winter Market, and Christmas by the Stream at London Scaffold. Each market has its unique appeal and attractions, so it merits visiting a couple to get the full insight.

Chapter 7: Food and Drink

London is a city of culinary joys, offering an inconceivable assortment of food and drink that takes care of each and every taste and financial plan. From traditional British dishes to global cuisine, London's food scene is a must-encounter for any guest. Here is a speedy manual for what makes eating and drinking in London so extraordinary.

Traditional British Fare

At the point when in London, it is an unquestionable necessity to attempt traditional British food. Exemplary dishes like fried fish and French fries, a good plate of battered fish presented with thick-cut fries, are tracked down in numerous pubs and eateries. Another most loved is the Sunday cook, highlighting broil meat, sheep, or chicken, presented with vegetables, broil potatoes, and

Yorkshire pudding. Remember to attempt a full English breakfast, which incorporates eggs, bacon, frankfurters, beans, and toast, frequently with dark pudding and barbecued tomatoes.

Afternoon Tea

Afternoon tea is a quintessentially British encounter. This wonderful custom incorporates a determination of finely fermented teas, finger sandwiches, scones with coagulated cream and jam, and a collection of baked goods and cakes. Numerous lodgings and bistros offer afternoon tea, with places like The Ritz and Fortnum and Bricklayer giving an especially rich encounter.

Diverse Global Cuisine

London's food scene is unbelievably diverse, mirroring the city's multicultural populace. You can track down cuisine from practically every country. Indian food is especially well known, with Block Path being popular for its variety of curry houses. Chinatown offers delightful Chinese food, while regions like Brixton and Shoreditch brag a variety of Caribbean, African, and Center Eastern diners.

Street Food and Markets

For a more easygoing feasting experience, London's street food and markets are phenomenal. Ward Market is one of the city's most seasoned and most prestigious food markets, offering all that from new produce to connoisseur street food. Camden Market is another area of interest, known for its diverse blend of food slows down serving global flavors. Markets like these are perfect for attempting various foods in a single spot.

Pubs and Drinks

London's pubs are a basic piece of its social scene. Partake in a 16 ounces of traditional British lager or juice in a comfortable, memorable bar. Numerous pubs likewise serve food, offering exemplary British dishes and solace food. For something more current, London has a flourishing mixed drink bar scene, with places like Soho and Shoreditch offering stylish bars and creative drinks.

Affordable Eats

Eating out in London doesn't need to be costly. There are a lot of affordable choices, from easygoing bistros and food trucks to chain cafés and ethnic restaurants. Places like Pret a Trough and Leon offer solid, speedy dinners, while food courts like Boxpark give various affordable, scrumptious choices.

Traditional British Cuisine

Traditional British cuisine could not necessarily get the spotlight, yet brimming with good dishes have been cherished for ages. These dinners are straightforward, encouraging, and frequently mirror the nation's set of experiences, environment, and horticultural practices.

One of the most notable British feasts is fried fish and French fries. This dish, frequently delighted in on a Friday night, highlights battered and broiled fish, generally cod or haddock, presented with thick-cut fries (called "chips" in the UK). It's normally joined by soft peas and a sprinkle of salt and vinegar. Fried fish and French fries became well known in the nineteenth hundred years as a modest and filling feast for common individuals.

Another notable British dish is the Sunday cook. Traditionally served on Sundays, this feast comprises of broiled meat (like hamburger, chicken, sheep, or pork), potatoes, and different vegetables like carrots, peas, and parsnips. The meal is typically presented with Yorkshire pudding (a flavorful, prepared hitter), sauce, and some of the time stuffing. The Sunday cook is something beyond a feast; it's a social custom where families assemble to partake in food together.

Breakfast in England is one more feast established in custom. The full English breakfast, or "cook," is a significant beginning to the day, including eggs, bacon, frankfurters, heated beans, tomatoes, mushrooms, and toast. Here and there, dark pudding (a kind of blood frankfurter) and hash browns are added. A feast was generally eaten by laborers before a drawn out day of work, giving a lot of energy.

Evening tea is maybe the most quintessentially British culinary practice. While it's all the more a social event as opposed to a dinner, it includes a determination of sensitive sandwiches (like cucumber or egg salad), scones with coagulated cream and jam, and a variety of cakes and baked goods. The custom traces all the way back to the nineteenth century when it became well known among the privileged societies, and it stays an image of British friendliness.

One can't discuss British cuisine without referencing pies. Whether exquisite or sweet, pies are a British staple. Shepherd's pie (made with minced sheep and finished off with pureed potatoes) and bungalow pie (the equivalent yet with meat) are traditional solace food sources. On the better side, fruity dessert, remedy tart, and mince pies (loaded up with flavored natural product) are famous pastries.

Another traditional dish is bangers and crush, which essentially implies hotdogs presented with pureed potatoes and sauce. This modest dish is a #1 in British bars and homes the same, known for its delightful and direct flavors.

Stews and soups likewise have a long history in British cuisine, with hamburger stew and Lancashire hotpot (a sluggish cooked dish of fundamentals) being exemplary models. These feasts are ideal for England's in many cases cold and clammy climate, offering warmth and solace.

International Flavors

Envision finding a spot at a table and taking a chomp of food that transports you to one more region of the planet. This is the wizardry of worldwide flavors. These flavors are the extraordinary preferences and blends of fixings that address various societies and customs from around the globe. Each dish recounts an account of the spot it comes from, offering a sample of history, geology, and the manner in which individuals carry on with their lives.

The Zest of Life: What Makes Global Flavors Extraordinary?

Each culture has own approach to cooking and utilizing fixings are normal in its locale. For instance, in India, flavors like cumin, coriander, and turmeric are fundamental in making the strong kinds of curries and masalas. Interestingly, Italian food is known for its utilization of new spices like basil and oregano, joined with tomatoes, olive oil, and garlic to make rich pasta sauces and pizzas.

Global flavors frequently emerge from the normal assets accessible in various regions. Waterfront nations like Japan and Greece, where fish is plentiful, have created dishes that feature fish. In tropical locales, organic products like mangoes, coconuts, and pineapples assume a significant part in cooking. In the mean time, nations with colder environments, similar to Russia, depend on root vegetables, grains, and saved meats to make generous and warming feasts.

An Excursion All over the Planet in Your Kitchen

Today, it's more straightforward than at any other time to encounter worldwide flavors without leaving your home. Grocery stores stock fixings from around the world, and innumerable recipes are accessible on the web. You can make Mexican tacos with only a couple of basic fixings like tortillas, beans, cheddar, and salsa, or take a stab at Japanese sushi, utilizing rice, ocean growth, and new fish.

Attempting global flavors isn't just tomfoolery yet additionally a method for finding out about various societies. At the point when you cook or taste food from another country, you get a brief look into the existences of individuals who made those dishes. For example, the zesty, tasty dishes of Thailand mirror the nation's warm environment and the significance of new fixings. Also, French cooking, known for its rich sauces and sensitive baked goods, shows the nation's adoration for class and high end food.

The General Language of Food

Quite possibly of the most gorgeous thing about worldwide flavors is their capacity to unite individuals. Food is a widespread language that everybody can comprehend. Sharing a feast from another culture can be a method for interfacing with others, commend variety, and fabricate companionships. Whether you're eating Italian pizza with companions, getting a charge out of Indian curry at an eatery, or cooking Chinese sautéed food at home, you're partaking in a worldwide custom of sharing and getting a charge out of food.

Food Markets

London is a city bursting with culture, history, and, importantly, food. One of the best ways to experience the city's rich culinary landscape is by visiting its many food markets. These markets aren't just places to buy groceries—they are vibrant, bustling hubs where you can taste foods from around the world, meet local producers, and experience the unique character of different neighborhoods.

Borough Market: A Food Lover's Paradise

Borough Market, located near London Bridge, is one of the city's oldest and most famous food markets. It's been around for over 1,000 years, and today it's a haven for food enthusiasts. When you walk through Borough Market, you're greeted by the smells of freshly baked bread, sizzling street food, and aromatic spices. The market is home to dozens of stalls selling everything from organic fruits and vegetables to artisanal cheeses and gourmet chocolates.

One of the best things about Borough Market is the variety of food available. You can grab a juicy burger, try traditional British pies, or indulge in sweet treats like doughnuts or brownies. The market also offers plenty of samples, so you can taste your way through the stalls before deciding what to buy.

A picture of an ice cream stall at Borough Market

Camden Market: A Feast of Flavors

Camden Market, located in the lively Camden Town, is another must-visit for food lovers. Camden is known for its alternative vibe, and the market reflects this with its diverse range of street food. Here, you can find flavors from every corner of the globe. Whether you're in the mood for Mexican tacos, Japanese sushi, or Ethiopian injera, Camden Market has it all.

The market is also famous for its vegan and vegetarian options. You'll find stalls serving plant-based burgers, vegan ice cream, and fresh juices. Camden Market is a great place to grab a bite to eat while exploring the area's quirky shops and live music venues.

Spitalfields Market: Tradition Meets Trendy

Spitalfields Market, located in East London, combines tradition with a modern twist. The market dates back to the 17th century but has been transformed into a trendy destination where food, fashion, and art come together. At Spitalfields, you can enjoy a range of gourmet street food while browsing through stalls selling handmade crafts and vintage clothing.

The food here is a blend of traditional and contemporary. You can try classic British dishes like fish and chips or dive into international cuisine with options like Spanish paella, Lebanese wraps, or Italian pizza. Spitalfields is also a great spot for brunch, with many stalls offering delicious pastries, coffee, and fresh smoothies.

Maltby Street Market: A Hidden Gem

Maltby Street Market is a smaller, more intimate market located in Bermondsey, south of the River Thames. While it may not be as famous as Borough or Camden, it's a favorite among locals and those in the know. The market is tucked away under railway arches, giving it a cozy and charming atmosphere.

Maltby Street Market is the perfect place to spend a relaxed weekend morning. The market's stalls offer a carefully curated selection of food, from gourmet grilled cheese sandwiches to craft beers and freshly baked pastries. It's also a great place to chat with vendors and learn more about the food you're eating, as many of the stallholders are passionate about their products.

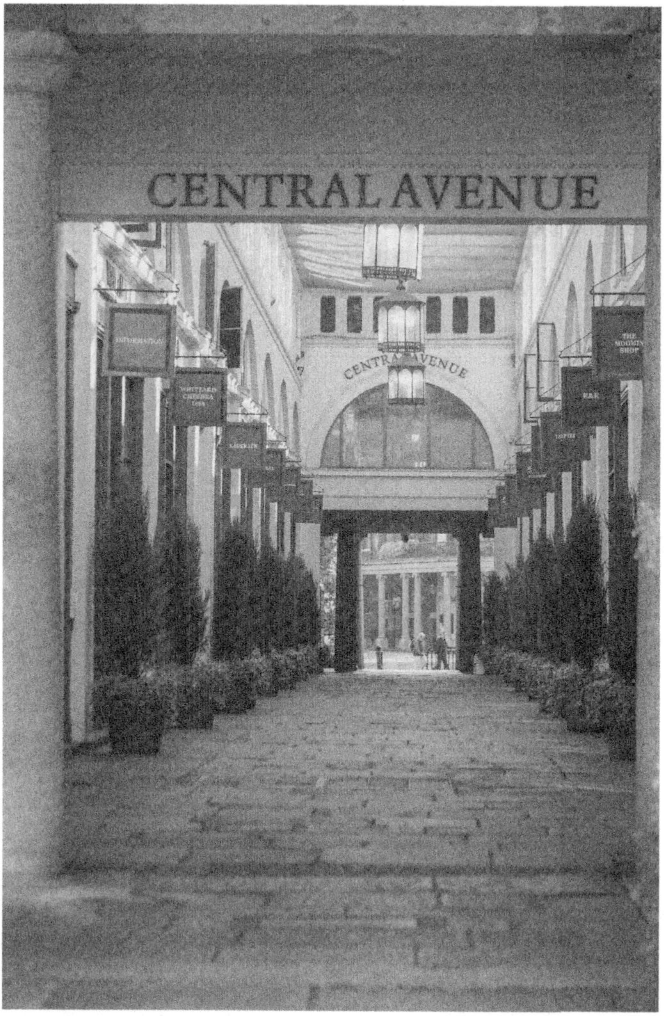
CENTRAL AVENUE

Chapter:8 Shopping

London is perhaps of the best city on the planet for shopping. It's where you can find everything from extravagance brands to eccentric market slows down, making it a fantasy objective for any individual who loves to shop.

Famous Shopping Areas

One of the most notable shopping roads in London is Oxford Road. It's loaded with large name stores like Selfridges, Zara, and H&M, offering all that from high design to reasonable dress. Not far off, Official Road is home to additional upscale stores, including Hamleys, the incredibly popular toy store.

Assuming you're into extravagance shopping, go to Bond Road. This road is fixed with architect stores like Chanel, Louis Vuitton, and Tiffany and Co. It's the ideal spot to indulge yourself with something uniquely great.

Markets and Unique Finds

London's markets are a mother lode for those searching for something unique. Camden Market is famous for its elective design, classic finds, and road food. It's an energetic spot where you can go through hours perusing and finding cool things.

Portobello Street Market in Notting Slope is another must-visit. It's particularly known for collectibles, however you can likewise track down garments, gems, and souvenirs. The market extends for a significant distance, so there's a lot to investigate.

Department Stores and Malls

For an across the board shopping experience, London's department stores are unbelievable. Harrods in Knightsbridge is an extravagance shopping objective including creator dress to luxurious cuisine. Regardless of whether you purchase anything, it merits visiting just to see the grandeur of the store.

Westfield London in White City is one of the biggest shopping malls in Europe. With north of 300 stores, including high road and extravagance brands, it's an incredible spot to go through a day shopping, feasting, and in any event, getting a film.

Souvenirs and Local Crafts

No excursion to London is finished without getting a few souvenirs. You can find exemplary gifts like tea, chocolates, and English themed things at numerous traveller shops across the city. For something more unique, look at local specialty shops and markets where you can purchase handmade merchandise, craftsmanship, and idiosyncratic tokens.

Famous Shopping Streets

London is home to probably the most popular shopping streets on the planet, each offering a one of a kind encounter for customers. Whether you're after very good quality style, in vogue stores, or eccentric finds, these streets have everything.

Oxford Street

Oxford Street is London's most renowned shopping street and one of the most active in Europe. Extending over a mile and a portion of, it's fixed with in excess of 300 shops, including notable retail chains like Selfridges and famous high-street brands like Zara and H&M. Oxford Street is the spot to go in the event that you're looking for the most stylish trend patterns or simply need to encounter the buzzing about of London shopping.

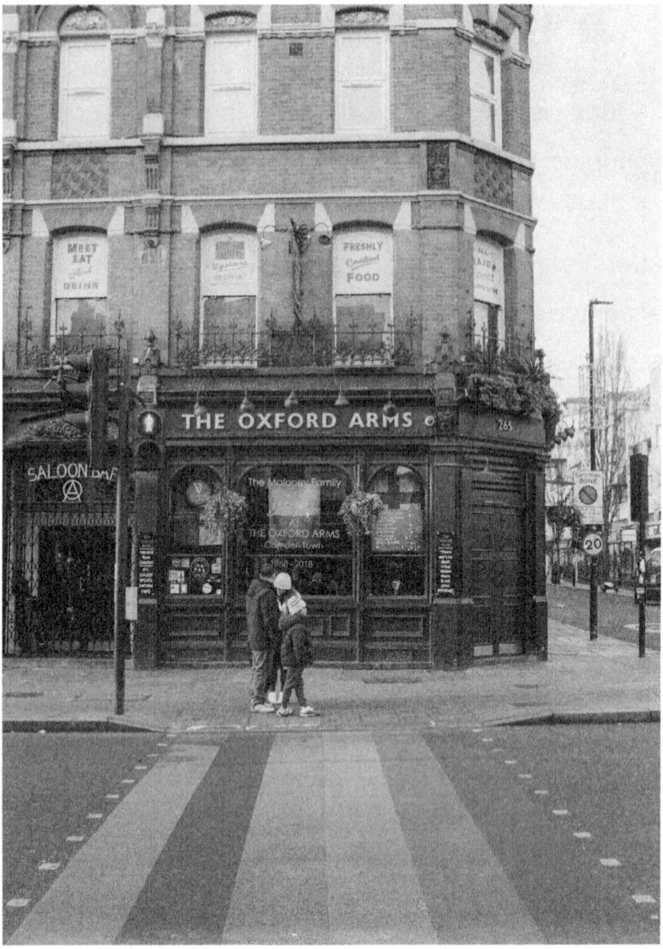
THE OXFORD ARMS
The Maloney Family
THE OXFORD ARMS
FRESHLY

Regent Street

Not far off from Oxford Street is Regent Street, known for its shocking engineering and lofty stores. This street is home to Freedom, a renowned retail chain with its wonderful Tudor-style working, as well as lead stores for brands like Apple and Hamleys, the world's most established toy store. Regent Street offers a more upscale shopping experience contrasted with Oxford Street, with a blend of extravagance and high-street brands.

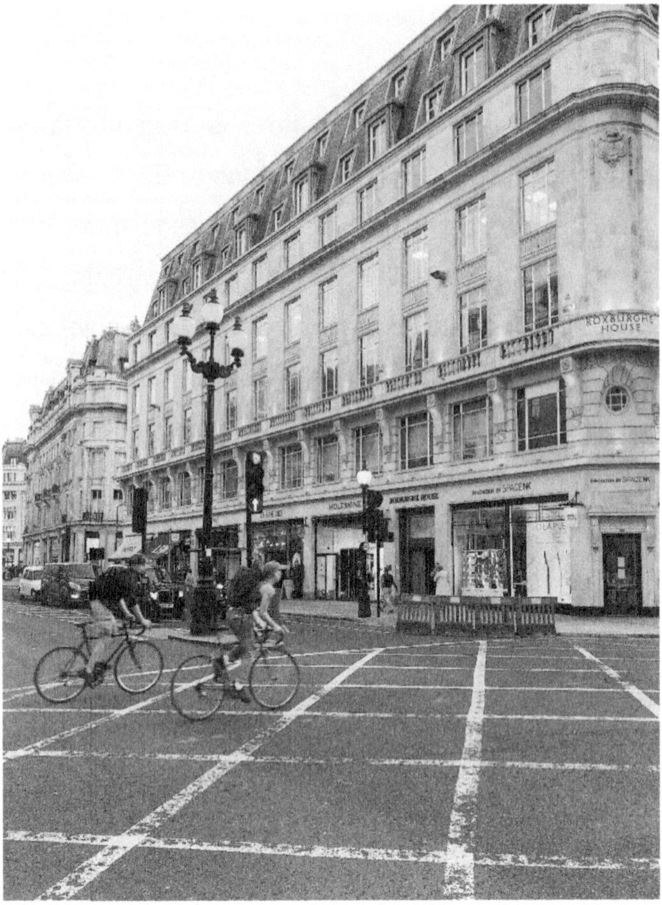
ROXBURGHE
HOUSE

Bond Street

For those looking for extravagance, Bond Street is the spot to be. This restrictive street is fixed with top of the line originator stores like Louis Vuitton, Chanel, and Gucci. It's where the rich and well known go out on the town to shop, and regardless of whether you're simply window shopping, the exquisite shows and refined climate make it worth a visit. Bond Street is likewise home to a portion of London's best gem dealers, like Cartier and Tiffany and Co..

Carnaby Street

Carnaby Street, situated in the popular Soho area, is well known for its energetic and autonomous design scene. During the 1960s, it was the focal point of London's design unrest, it actually has a young, imaginative energy today. The street is loaded up with free stores, idiosyncratic shops, and cool cafés. It's the ideal spot to track down something extraordinary and unique, from classic apparel to state of the art design.

Covent Garden

Covent Garden is something other than a shopping street; it's an entire region loaded up with shops, markets, and street entertainers. The Covent Garden Market is the core of the region, offering a blend of hand tailored makes, creator merchandise, and exceptional gifts. The close by streets are home to different stores, from enormous name brands like Mulberry to autonomous shops. Covent Garden is likewise known for its dynamic climate, with a lot of bistros and cafés to loosen up in following a day of shopping.

King's Road

King's Road in Chelsea is one more renowned shopping objective known for its stylish and popular energy. During the 1960s and 70s, it was the focal point of the London style scene, and today it's home to a blend of top of the line shops, inside plan shops, and design stores. King's Road is the spot to go for a more easygoing, slick shopping experience.

Chapter 9: Day Trips from London

London is an intriguing city with a lot to see and do, yet one of its incredible benefits is its vicinity to other entrancing objections. On the off chance that you have a day in excess, there are a few extraordinary spots you can visit simply a short excursion away from the capital. Here are the absolute greatest road trips from London.

Windsor

Simply an hour from London via train, Windsor is home to the renowned Windsor Palace, one of the authority homes of the English royal family. The palace is the most established and biggest involved palace on the planet, and you can investigate its fantastic rooms, shocking St. George's Sanctuary, and lovely nurseries. Windsor itself is a beguiling town with a lot of shops, eateries, and beautiful strolls along the Waterway Thames.

Oxford

Known as the "City of Dreaming Towers," Oxford is eminent for its esteemed college, which is one of the most established on the planet. A visit to Oxford permits you to investigate memorable universities, for example, Christ Church, where scenes from the Harry Potter films were shot. You can likewise meander through the Bodleian Library, quite possibly the most seasoned library in Europe, and partake in a relaxed dropkick on the Stream Cherwell.

Bath

Bath is a wonderful Georgian city renowned for its very much safeguarded Roman baths, which date back almost 2,000 years. The city's shocking design, including the Imperial Sickle and Bath Nunnery, makes it an UNESCO World Legacy site. Bath is likewise known for its normal natural aquifers, and you can encounter the loosening up waters at the advanced Thermae Bath Spa. The excursion to Bath from London requires around 90 minutes via train.

Stonehenge

Stonehenge is perhaps the most popular ancient landmark on the planet, and it's simply a two-hour drive from London. This baffling stone circle, accepted to have been built close to a long time back, keeps on fascinating guests with its old beginnings and reason. A visit to Stonehenge regularly incorporates a stop at the close by Salisbury Church, home to one of the first duplicates of the Magna Carta.

Cambridge

Like Oxford, Cambridge is known for its incredibly popular college. The city is pleasant, with its notable universities, lavish green spaces, and the Waterway Cam moving through the core of it. A well known movement in Cambridge is drop-kicking on the waterway, where you can skim past lovely school structures and under beguiling extensions. The excursion from London to Cambridge requires about an hour via train.

Brighton

For a shoreline escape, make a beeline for Brighton on the south coast, simply an hour from London via train. Brighton is an exuberant city with a blend of conventional oceanside attractions and present day culture. You can walk around the Brighton Wharf, investigate the eccentric shops in The Paths, and visit the staggering Imperial Structure, a previous regal royal residence with a remarkable, fascinating plan. Brighton is additionally known for its dynamic expressions scene and energetic nightlife.

Windsor

Oxford

Cambridge

Bath

Stonehenge

Brighton

Chapter 10: Practical Information

London is a vibrant and bustling city that attracts millions of visitors each year. To make the most of your trip, it's important to know some practical information about getting around, staying safe, and managing everyday essentials. Here's a quick guide to help you navigate London with ease.

Currency and Money

The currency in London is the British Pound Sterling (GBP). You'll find plenty of ATMs around the city, and credit/debit cards are widely accepted, including for small purchases. However, it's always a good idea to carry some cash, especially for markets or small shops that might be cash-only. If you need to exchange money, avoid doing so at airports, where rates are often less favorable.

Getting Around

London has an extensive and well-connected public transport system. The London Underground (Tube) is the quickest way to get around the city, with 11 lines covering most areas. Buses are another great option, especially for shorter journeys or if you want to see the city as you travel. Oyster cards and contactless payment cards are the easiest ways to pay for public transport. These cards can be used on the Tube, buses, trams, and even some riverboat services.

For those who prefer walking, central London is very walkable, with many of the major attractions located close to each other. Taxis and ride-sharing services like Uber are also available, but they can be more expensive, especially during peak times.

Weather and What to Wear

London weather can be unpredictable, so it's wise to be prepared. The city has a temperate climate, with mild winters and cool summers. Rain is common, so bringing an umbrella or a waterproof jacket is a good idea. Layering your clothing is also helpful, as temperatures can vary throughout the day. Comfortable shoes are essential, especially if you plan on doing a lot of walking.

Health and Safety

London is generally a safe city, but it's always important to stay aware of your surroundings. Keep an eye on your belongings, especially in crowded areas like public transport and tourist hotspots. Emergency services are efficient, and in case of any issues, dial 999 for emergencies or 111 for non-urgent medical advice. Pharmacies are widely available for any over-the-counter medications or health needs.

Communication and Internet

English is the official language in London, and most people will speak it fluently. Public Wi-Fi is available in many places, including cafes, restaurants, and public spaces like parks. If you need to stay connected, consider getting a local SIM card or an international roaming plan for your mobile phone.

Tipping and Etiquette

Tipping is customary in London, but it's not as mandatory as in some other countries. In restaurants, a 10-15% tip is typical if service isn't included in the bill. For taxis, rounding up to the nearest pound or adding a small tip is appreciated. Londoners are generally polite, so it's a good idea to say "please" and "thank you," and queue (line up) when waiting for services like buses or in shops.

Emergency Contacts

It's always helpful to know the local emergency numbers. In London, the number to call for any emergency, such as needing the police, fire service, or an ambulance, is 999. If you have a non-emergency medical issue, you can call 111 for advice. Additionally, it's good to have your country's embassy contact information handy in case you need assistance.

Chapter 11: Useful Phrases

When visiting London, having a few key phrases under your belt can make your experience smoother and more enjoyable. While English is the primary language spoken, Londoners use some phrases and expressions that might be new to visitors. Here's a quick guide to some useful phrases that will help you navigate conversations in the city.

Common Greetings

- "Hello" and "Hi": These are the standard greetings you'll hear everywhere. Londoners might also say "Hey" in a casual setting.
- "Cheers": This is a versatile word that can mean "thank you," "goodbye," or just a friendly acknowledgment.
- "How are you?" or "You alright?": These are common ways to ask someone how

they're doing. "You alright?" is particularly common in London and is just a casual way to say "How's it going?"

Asking for Directions

- "Excuse me, could you tell me how to get to...?": This is a polite way to ask for directions.
- "Which way is...?": Another simple way to ask for directions.
- "Is it far?": Useful if you want to know if your destination is within walking distance.
- "Where's the nearest Tube station?": The Tube is London's underground train system, and asking this will help you find the closest station.

Ordering Food and Drinks

- "I'll have...": Use this when ordering something at a restaurant or café. For example, "I'll have a coffee, please."
- "Can I get the bill, please?": This is how you ask for the check after a meal.

313

- "To go" or "Takeaway": If you want your food or drink to take with you, use either of these phrases.

Polite Expressions

- "Please" and "Thank you": These are essential for polite interactions. Londoners appreciate good manners.
- "Sorry": In London, you'll hear "sorry" a lot, even when someone isn't really at fault. It's often used just to be polite, like if you accidentally bump into someone or need to get someone's attention.
- "Pardon?" or "Sorry?": If you didn't hear or understand something, use these phrases to ask someone to repeat what they said.

Getting Around

- "Single" or "Return": When buying a ticket for the Tube or bus, you'll need to say whether you want a "single" (one-way) or "return" (round trip) ticket.

- "Where's the nearest cashpoint?": "Cashpoint" is the British term for an ATM.
- "Mind the gap": You'll hear this phrase on the Tube. It's a reminder to watch your step when boarding or exiting the train.

Slang and Local Terms

- "Loo": This is the British word for the bathroom or restroom. You might ask, "Where's the loo?"
- "Brilliant": This word is used to express approval or excitement, similar to "great" or "awesome."
- "Fancy": This word can mean "like" or "want," as in "Do you fancy a cup of tea?"

British Slang and Idioms

When you visit the UK, you might hear some words and expressions that sound unfamiliar or unusual, even if you speak English. British slang and idioms add color and personality to the language, and understanding them can help you feel more connected to British culture. Here's a quick guide to some common British slang and idioms that you might come across.

Common British Slang

- "Cheeky": This word is used to describe someone who is playful or a bit mischievous, but in a fun, harmless way. For example, if someone takes the last biscuit without asking, you might say, "That was a bit cheeky!"
- "Chuffed": If someone says they're "chuffed," it means they're very pleased or happy about something. For example, "I'm chuffed to bits about my new job."

- "Dodgy": This word is used to describe something that seems suspicious or not quite right. For example, "That deal sounds a bit dodgy to me."
- "Gobsmacked": If you're "gobsmacked," you're completely shocked or amazed. For example, "I was gobsmacked when I won the lottery."
- "Knackered": This is a common way to say that you're very tired. After a long day of sightseeing, you might say, "I'm absolutely knackered."
- "Mate": This is a friendly term for a friend or someone you're on good terms with. For example, "How's it going, mate?"
- "Loo": This is the British term for the bathroom or toilet. You might hear someone ask, "Where's the loo?"
- "Bangers and mash": This is a classic British dish made of sausages and mashed potatoes. It's a popular comfort food.

Popular British Idioms

- "It's raining cats and dogs": This idiom means it's raining very heavily. You might hear it when the weather takes a turn for the worse.
- "Piece of cake": If something is a "piece of cake," it means it's very easy to do. For example, "That test was a piece of cake."
- "Cost an arm and a leg": This phrase means something is very expensive. For example, "That new car must have cost an arm and a leg."
- "Break the ice": This idiom is used when you do something to make people feel more comfortable, especially in a social setting. For example, "Telling a joke is a great way to break the ice."
- "Bite the bullet": This phrase means to do something difficult or unpleasant that you've been avoiding. For example, "I didn't want to go to the dentist, but I had to bite the bullet."
- "Under the weather": If someone says they're "under the weather," it means they're feeling unwell. For example, "I'm feeling a bit under the weather today."
- "Throw in the towel": This idiom means to give up or quit something. For example,

"After trying to fix the computer for hours, I finally threw in the towel."

Chapter 12:. Maps and Guides

When visiting a new city like London, having a good map or guide can make all the difference. Whether you're exploring on foot, using public transport, or planning your itinerary, maps and guides are essential tools to help you get around and make the most of your trip.

The Importance of Maps

A map is a visual representation of a place that shows you where things are and how to get from one place to another. In London, maps are especially useful because the city is large and can be confusing to navigate, especially for first-time visitors.

• City Maps: These maps show the overall layout of London, including major roads, landmarks, and neighbourhoods. They're helpful for getting a sense of where you are and how far you need to go.

• Tube Maps: London's underground train system, known as the Tube, is one of the best ways to get around the city. The Tube map is a simplified guide that shows all the train lines and stations. It's essential for figuring out which line to take and where to transfer if needed.

The Role of Guides

Guides provide more detailed information than maps alone. They often include tips, recommendations, and background information that can enhance your experience.

• Travel Guides: These are books or pamphlets that cover everything a traveller needs to know about London. They often include maps, but they also offer information on popular attractions, restaurants, shopping areas, and cultural tips. A good travel guide can help you plan your trip and make sure you don't miss any must-see spots.

• Walking Guides: If you enjoy exploring on foot, walking guides can be very helpful. They provide suggested routes, pointing out interesting landmarks, hidden gems, and scenic paths. These guides are great for experiencing the city at a slower pace and discovering places you might not find on your own.

• Mobile Apps: In today's digital age, many travellers use mobile apps as their primary guide. Apps like Google Maps or Citymapper provide real-time navigation, directions, and information about public transport. They're convenient because they're always up-to-date and can adjust to your current location.

Why You Need Both

While guides give you ideas and recommendations, maps help you figure out how to get to those places. Having both means you're prepared for anything. For example, a travel guide might recommend a visit to the British Museum, and your map will show you how to get there by Tube or on foot.

City Map

https://www.visitacity.com/en/london/attractions

Printed in Great Britain
by Amazon